The Return of Ms. Rose

Stephanie K. Randall

For the Readers of
Living Fast

Copyright 2013 by Stephanie K. Randall

All rights reserved.

ACKNOWLEDGEMENTS

As I would in any other instance, I have to give honor to my Lord and savior Jesus Christ. Without Him I am capable of nothing, and I am aware of that. I do not take His blessings for granted, and I thank Him for them all, including this book. I want to thank my mother of course, Mrs. Bridgett Tucker for being a strong motivating force in my life. When I need advice, I call her. When I need comfort I lean on her. I thank God for giving me a mother that I can always depend on and that supports me in everything I do. When I figured out that being an author was what I wanted to do with my life, she never made me feel like I was being foolish. To anyone out there who still has a mother to love and respect, make sure that you do that. There is nothing like the love you get from your mother. Throughout the process of writing this book, I have lost so much. There have been times when I just wanted to throw in the towel. But then I would talk to my cousin Lisa Holley, and she would give me so many words of encouragement. She has been there from day one, cheering me on, encouraging me to be great. I couldn't ask for a better cousin. I want to thank my cousin Nina Roots for pushing my book like it was her own (lol). I want to thank my children Sanaa and Shiloh for giving me two more reasons to strive for excellence. At the end of the day, I'm doing this for them. I have to set the tone. I tell Sanaa all the time to take pride in herself and to be great in whatever she does, so it's only natural that I at least try to take my own advice. When Shiloh becomes old enough to understand I will tell her the same thing. I also want to thank my God mother Mary Annette Whitley for keeping me in prayer. For every storm that I went through she always had an encouraging word. I would like to thank my good friend Frankie Jones for encouraging me even when we both are busy and trying to grind it out. I would like to thank my manager and good friend Diamond K for stepping in and helping me with anything that I need. I want to thank Kevin B. Watkins of Classic Image.ry for the beautiful picture on the cover. I also want to thank Skarr Akbar for designing an amazing cover. And last but certainly not least I want to thank everyone who read Living Fast and who kept asking for the sequel. Yall just don't know how good it feels to know that people feel and love my work. I'm not only writing for entertainment, I'm writing to send a message. Every book has a message, and I am trying to connect with everybody on different levels. Prayerfully you guys see it. Thanks again and I love you all. Xoxoxo...... The best is yet to come.

TABLE OF CONTENTS

CHAPTER 1: I'm Back..1
CHAPTER 2: Easy Like Sunday Morning.........................3
CHAPTER 3: Stepping In...14
CHAPTER 4: Trust..26
CHAPTER 5: Baby Deon..29
CHAPTER 6: It Will Get Better...49
CHAPTER 7: Crazy...54
CHAPTER 8: Crazier..62
CHAPTER 9: Mrs. Clause..69
CHAPTER 10: Love, Celebration, and Scandal................80
CHAPTER 11: The Showdown..88
CHAPTER 12: Winners..95
CHAPTER 13: Youth..100
CHAPTER 14: I Don't Like Andrew................................105
CHAPTER 15: It's a Celebration.....................................114
CHAPTER 16: Rose Pedals and Birthday Betrayal...........123
CHAPTER 17: Attempting to Carry On..........................131
CHAPTER 18: Down Pour...136
CHAPTER 19: Finding out Where I Came From............147
CHAPTER 20: Tuscany and Decisions............................154
CHAPTER 21: Juan Sanchez...166

CHAPTER 1: I'm Back

"Awww don't cry my baby," I said in the sweetest voice that I could.

I had never been happier to get up at three in the morning. I cradled her in my arms and gave her my breast. I was a mother for the third time. Her birthday is December twenty fifth, I like to call her the best Christmas gift ever. I named her Summer, because when I gave birth to her, she came out so bright and full of life. She was so sweet and cuddly even at three a.m. and the perfect addition to my family. Having her was my chance to do it right from the beginning. I had to make sure that I raised her right from the start, and that is what I was doing. I was clean and sober, and most of all, I had found a church home and I finally given my life to Christ. If only I could get my filthy mouth a little more under control. Hahahaha. But, I'm still a work in progress. I was moving in the right direction, and I couldn't be happier with my new way of life.

Oh shucks I'm sorry I'm being so rude. It's me Rose. Well Ms. Rose is what I like to call myself. Yall remember me? How yall doing? Well let me fill yall in on what's been going on with me. I went and got my Bachelor's degree in early childhood education, and now I own my own daycare center. I love being a business owner. Instead of indulging in unhealthy behaviors to cope with stress, I write poetry and read my Bible. That sounds strange coming from me right? Trust me I know, but change is good especially when it's for the better. I know yall are wondering where's Deon right? Well he ain't gone nowhere. Hahahaha but seriously though, he's my husband now. We got married about two years ago, and let me tell you the wedding was so beautiful. Bling everywhere. All white everything. Plus the fattest rock I have ever seen is sitting on my ring finger, along with a sparkly wedding band. The reception was filled with laughter, dancing, and plenty of food too. Lil Franko and Deon's son, Deonte' were the ring bearers, and Miracle was the flower girl of course. Life is definitely good now, and I don't take anything for granted. My husband loves me, and I love him too. I'm loving the married life. I love my whole family unit. Everything is falling into place. Miracle and Lil Franko are well adjusted to life with me as well. When I had Summer, they were nine and ten, and I had them both enrolled into an excellent Christian based private school. I made sure that they wanted for nothing and I showered them with attention. My kids are my world, they mean everything to me. Nothing makes me happier than to see them happy.

    So at this point in my life, all I'm trying to do is stay focused and be the best mother and wife that I can be. I realize that I have been blessed with another chance, so going back to how I used to be isn't even an option. With that being said, let me take yall a little deeper into what's been going on. Strap on your seat belt though, because even though life is much better it isn't always rainbows and glitter.

CHAPTER 2: Easy Like Sunday Morning

I woke up feeling great. It was Sunday morning, one of the best days of the week in my eyes. Church, and then a flight to wherever Deon was playing when there was an away game was the schedule for football season. I got out of bed, got fresh, then got in the kitchen and did what I loved to do. I made a big breakfast too: scrambled cheese eggs, fried potatoes, homemade waffles, grits, fresh fruit, and sausage links. I set the table and placed two pitchers of juice in the center. No more than two minutes after I was done, I heard cries coming from the baby monitor. I looked at it and there was Summer rolling around the crib, wanting to be tended to. I went back upstairs to her room and took her out of her crib.

"Good morning my beautiful baby," I said to her.

She responded with a big smile. I hugged her, then laid her on the changing table and changed her diaper. Then I picked her back up and went down the hall. I stopped at Miracle's room.

"Get up Boo it's time for breakfast," I said to her. " Go wake your brothers up. And make sure you tell them not to come down my stairs until they brush their teeth and was their faces."

"OK," Miracle said.

Miracle being the oldest, loved to be in charge. So I always gave her that job. I went back downstairs and put Summer in her high chair, and began to feed her some eggs. A few minutes later all I heard was thumping. It sounded like a herd of elephants coming down the stairs. But it wasn't. It was just those hungry kids racing to the table to get some of my delicious breakfast. They rushed to the table and sat down. Miracle was the last one.

"Haha Miracle is a rotten egg," Deonte' laughed.

"Shut up dummy," she said.

"OK now what did I say about the name calling?" I butted in.

"She just mad she smells like a rotten egg," Lil Franko laughed.

Those kids were something else. I always had fun with them, and they loved when Deon's son came over and stayed for the weekend. You couldn't even tell that they were step brothers and sisters. They had an awesome relationship with each other.

"OK yall less talking and more eating. We have to get ready for church and Man Man your mother will be here in a little while to pick you up.

"Aww man! I wish I could stay longer! My mother be geekin," he said.

"Man Man what did I tell you about your mouth? That is your mother so what she says goes," I said, even though I totally agreed with him.

Nevertheless, I had to make sure that he respected his mother, right or wrong. After they finished eating I sent everyone upstairs to take showers and get dressed. I washed all the dishes and tidied up the kitchen while Summer played with her toys in her play pen. After I was finished I took her upstairs with me and bathed her, then got her dressed.

"Awww look at Mommy baby!" I said.

I picked her up and held her tight. Summer was my pride and joy. It's something about having and infant that is so fulfilling. Babies are truly a gift from God. Her baby pink dress with matching headband made her even more loveable. I sat down on the bed and rocked her to sleep. After I laid her down I could finally get dressed. Thoughts of my Deon went through my head as I got myself ready. I really missed him and I couldn't wait to see him. He had been out of town all week, came home on Friday, and then was gone again on Saturday. That saying, "absence makes the heart grow fonder" is so true.

After I got dressed I made sure that everything was in Summer's diaper bag, and as I was zipping it up when I heard a car's horn beeping repeatedly from outside. I already knew who it was.

"Man Man get your stuff your mother is out side," I called out to him.

"OK," he answered back.

I put on my stilettos and walked out side to the front of my house. Trina sat in her car looking miserable as usual. I smiled inside my head. I had never seen a woman that was always mad. She was such a sad case.

"Where's Deon?" Trina asked full of salt.

"His flight just landed this morning, and he had to go straight to the stadium. Why wassup?" I asked.

"He was supposed to give me the money for Deonte's football equipment."

"Oh yea. He told me to tell you that he was gonna put it in Deonte's account tomorrow," I informed Trina.

"Why couldn't he just give me the money? Why am I gonna have to go through all that?" she asked.

"Go through all what? All you gotta do is go to the ATM and withdraw it. Or better yet just swipe the card," I said.

"I don't even know why he is giving you messages to give to me. That is me and his son. You don't have nothing to do with it," Trina remarked.

"Trina, I have three kids of my own. I ain't tryna be your son's mother. But you just gotta face the fact that Deon is my husband. I am his wife. So whether you like it or not, I'm gonna be in the picture. I don't know why he asked me to relay the message. Hmmm.. Maybe because he isn't here. But you can take that up with him."

Trina stared at me so hard that I thought her eyes were gonna pop out of her block ass head. So I figured she was trying to compete with me in a staring contest and yall know I'm a competitor so I damn sure wasn't going to let her win. Finally, she rolled her eyes and proceeded to talk out the side of her neck again.

"Well make sure you tell your husband to call me 'cuz I got a bone to pick with him. And where is my damn son? I thought I told yall to have him ready when you know I'm on my way to get him?"

I felt myself getting pissed off so I turned around and started to walk back in my front door. This ignorant idiot could sit outside in her car and talk to herself for all I cared because I wasn't gonna listen to her talk trash for too much longer. As I was walking away I could have sworn I heard this dummy say, "yea you better go in the house." Now see, this is how I know that God is real, and that he definitely had been working on me. I say this because if this had been a few years prior, I would've skipped down that driveway and snatched her through that car window. But since I did hear what she said, whether she wanted me to or not, I had to let her know a thing or two about a thing or two.

"Let me tell you something. I ain't never backed down from nobody. I'm not scared of you by a long shot honey. I just choose my battles wisely. 'Cuz as soon as I knock your teeth out you're gonna be trying to sue me. Trust me honey I ain't never been no dumb chick. But I will say this. You have been warned. When you come around this mutha fucker you better come around here with some respect 'cuz I definitely haven't forgot how to choke a bitch out. You got one more time to bring some drama to my home and I promise you that you will be leaving here on a stretcher."

"Yeah whatever," Trina said.

"Try it again and see how far you get," I responded.

Deonte' came out of the house with his overnight bag.

"Hey Ma," he called out to Trina.

"Hey Tay Tay," she called back out to him.

"See you later Rosie," he said before he gave me a hug.

"See you later Man Man," I said to him, kissing him on his forehead.

I never wanted Deonte' to call me Ms. Rose. It was too formal and it made me feel old. And I didn't want him to call me Mommy because he had a mother. So I told him to call me my nick name Rosie. When I first met Deonte' the first thing I noticed was his deep voice. It sounded like he was a grown man. So that's why I gave him the nick name, Man Man.

He got in the car and Trina backed up out of the driveway. I watched her leave. I wasn't gonna turn my back on her, you never turn your back on your enemy because you never know what they got on their mind. What was her problem anyway? Why did she feel the need to beef with me? When Deonte' was with us, he was well taken care of. I cared for him and loved him like he was my own. So why was she mad at me? That's when another lesson blossomed within me. You will never be pleasing in the sight of a salty ex. Never. She will always find a reason to dislike you if she isn't happy with her own situation. And from the looks of things, Trina was down right miserable. But since I was a woman, in the true meaning of the word I had to act accordingly. I couldn't stoop down to her level, because as soon as I slapped the taste out of her mouth, she would be trying to keep Deonte' away from us. I definitely didn't want to have any parts of Deon being unable to see his son. I knew that would really hurt him.

"Lord, what is wrong with that girl? She got me out here cussing on Sunday morning. All I'm trying to do is go to church and get my praise on and she ready to make me bust her ass with my church clothes on," I said before I went back in the house.

    I knew that was nothing but the devil trying to take me out of my element, trying to make me stay home from church. But nope, it wasn't gonna happen. I had a great week, my kids were healthy, my marriage was good, and I had plenty more things to be thankful for. There was no way that I was gonna let Lucifer stop me from going to give my God some thanks. So after I took a few deep breaths I went into my room and I shut my door. If this was not a good enough time for me to pray then I didn't know what was. I had been reminded of the scripture, Matthew 6:6; but you when you pray, enter into your secret closet, and when you have shut your door, pray to your Father which is in secret; and your Father which sees in secret shall reward you openly. So that's what I did. I got on my knees and I prayed. I prayed for strength and I prayed that God would keep me when I was being tried by the enemy. I prayed that He would keep His arms around me and mine. But most of all I thanked him for Him for his favor over my life. I thanked Him for taking a nobody and making her into a somebody. Once I said Amen, I got up from the floor feeling better than I had before I had to lean on Trina. That was just the result that I was looking for too.

So I went on about my Sunday with a smile on my face. Church was great, and once it was over I took the kids for a quick bite to eat, then we were on our way to the Raven's stadium to watch Deon play. The kids were always so excited to go to his games. Even though they lived with him, they never got tired of being around a "celebrity". I wished Deonte' could be with us. But Trina was so spiteful that when it was time for him to go home, it was time for him to go home. She never cared if he got to come to his father's games or not. Her cruel behavior really rubbed me the wrong way. She was so blessed that her son had a father that was eager to be in his life. She didn't know how it felt to have a son that was fatherless. Some people really took their blessings for granted, and she was one of them for sure.

As soon as the game was over my phone was ringing. I looked to see who it was. It was my Aunt Lucinda. I shifted Summer to the opposite hip before I answered.
"Hey Aunt Lucy," I said.
"Rosie I have had enough of that girl. I can't do it no more. I need some peace in my home!"
"Hold up. What's going on?"
"She won't listen to me. She stays out all night. She won't go to school. She is very disrespectful. She doesn't have any kind of respect for me. Got all kinds of boys calling here. She talks all kinds of ways out her mouth to me. I'm at my wits end with her," Aunt Lucinda vented.
"OK. Well this is what I will do. I'm gonna go online and pay for a ticket for the Greyhound. It's time for her to come stay with me. She only needs to pack a few bags. I will send for the rest of her stuff. I'm sick of this foolishness, I really am," I said.
"Alright then. I know she is gonna be upset she is not gonna want to leave her friends-"
"Aunt Lucy I don't care nothing 'bout her being upset. If she was that concerned about being with her friends then she would've got her act together. I have warned her too many

times. I'm done with the threats, it's time to make it a reality," I said.

"I know, I know. I'm just saying," Aunt Lucinda tried to rationalize.

"I know you tried. It's OK," I tried to reassure her. "But I think it's time for you to get some rest, and to be about you for a change. I got her. Let her know that she is coming up here with me."

It was time for me to take the burden off of my aunt. She had taken us in. She had raised my kids while I was running wild after my mother died. I was ready to take the load off of her. It was only right. After I got home and put my dinner on, I got online and paid for the bus ticket. After everything was confirmed I called my aunt and let her know what was going on. Violet was to be on her way to Baltimore on Sunday, which was only a week away. The plan was for her to get on the bus at six a.m., and she would be in Baltimore by two in the afternoon, just in time to catch the flight to Miami with us for Deon's game. Next up on the list was to make sure that it was OK with Deon. Well not to make sure it was OK, but to run it past him. I wasn't going to ask permission for my sister to come live with us. That was my sister, so I wasn't going to take no for an answer anyway.

Just as I had expected, Deon was OK with it. He was aware of the severity of the situation. He agreed that I needed to step in with Violet and that Aunt Lucinda deserved to have her life back. So for the rest of the week I got things ready for Violet to come. I turned one of the extra rooms into her room. I also researched a few public schools but I wasn't satisfied with any of them. I decided that I would put her in a private christian school. Violet needed guidance and structure, so I thought that type of school would be good for her. Finally I came across a school that I liked. I made an appointment for the Monday after she was scheduled to arrive in Baltimore to check the school out. If it was up to par, I would be ready to enroll her. I had gotten everything into place.

Sunday rolled back around and I was excited to start this new chapter in my life. I was ready for my little sister to come and live with me. So naturally, I was totally taken aback when I got a call from my aunt while I was on my way with the kids to church.
"Hey Rosie. I don't mean to bother you, I know you are probably at church," she responded after I answered.
"It's OK. I'm not there yet I'm on my way though. Why aren't you at church yet?"
"Violet never came home last night."
"What?" I asked even though I had heard what she said.
"Nope, she never came in. I just kept thinking that maybe she was trying to go out with a bang, but she never came home. She's still not here. I didn't even get ready for church because I was waiting on her," my aunt explained.
"Oh OK. I see what she's trying to do. Every time I send for her she thinks she is gonna run away. But I got something for her. I'm coming down there tomorrow. Don't tell her I'm coming," I said.
"Rosie I don't wanna inconvenience you, I know you got a lot going on."
"It's not an inconvenience. I will be there tomorrow."
"What if she still don't come back?"
"She will. Oh trust me, she will. Call me once she comes home," I replied.

Oh it was on now. She made me waste my money on getting everything together for her ungrateful ass. And she made me waste my time making all these arrangements for school. I took that as blatant disrespect, and I don't take disrespect lightly. She was definitely in the wrong. This teenage girl stuff had my little sister going wild. It was time to bring all that mess to a halt. I loved Violet too much to let her fall by the wayside.

The rest of the day went as usual. I went to church with the kids, then we caught a flight to Deon's game. I usually had a good time at Deon's games, but I was too distracted with thoughts of Violet. I couldn't help but wonder if her acting out was partly my fault. I mean it did take me years to get myself together, and when I finally did get my kids back I didn't take her with me. But it wasn't like I was just leaving her behind. I still sent money to Aunt Lucinda for whatever she needed. I went down to visit when I could, and I flew her to Baltimore for the holidays. I didn't abandon her. I just thought that it would benefit her to stay with my aunt since she was older and she didn't want to leave her friends. Never did I think that she would rebel to the level that she had. I was beginning to feel like this might be a little too much for me. Was I really equipped with the tools to raise a teenager? I mean look at me, look at all the things that I had done. Look at all the times that I had stumbled and all the wrong that I had been involved in? I mean I was only her sister, I wasn't her mother. How could I step in and make things right? I was really starting to have doubts. My heart was heavy.

      Then I started to think back to service that morning. The verses that the pastor had used for his sermon flashed over and over in my head.
Matthew 11:28 Come unto me, all that ye labour and are heavy laden, and I will give you rest. 29 Take my yoke upon you, and learn of me, for I am meek and lowly in heart: and ye shall find rest unto your souls. 30 For my yoke is easy, and my burden is light.

      I had already taken the first step which was accepting the call to discipleship. I had accepted him into my life. Now all I had to do was continue to follow Him, and He would take care of the rest. Nothing is too hard for God. As long as I was sincere in what I was doing with taking on the responsibility of my sister, everything would be OK. A wave of calm washed over me. It was going to be OK.

      After the game was over, we waited for Deon to get cleaned up, and then we went out for a late dinner to celebrate their victory. As we sat and ate it must've all of a sudden dawned on Deon that Violet wasn't with us.
"Where's V?" he asked me.
"She ran away," Miracle blurted out.

"What?" Deon asked.

"Yeah she left when she found out that she was supposed to be coming to Baltimore," I said.

"Woah. So what are you gonna do now?"

"Well Aunt Lucy called me while we were waiting for you. She said that she was back home. I already had got online and booked a flight to Virginia for tomorrow morning once she had told me that V had skipped out. I wasn't gonna give her a chance to run away every time she was supposed to catch the bus up to Baltimore. So I'm gonna go get her in the morning and bring her back to Baltimore with me. But I told Aunt Lucy not to tell her I was coming because I didn't want her to try to run again."

"Oh. So you're planning a surprise attack?" Deon joked.

"I guess you can call it that. So look. I need you to keep the kids with you and bring them back in town when you come back. I don't want to take them with me because I really don't know how Violet is gonna act."

"OK. That's cool with me. But don't they have school tomorrow?" Deon asked.

"Yea they do. But this is very important so I think it'll be OK for them to miss one day. They have great attendance so one day wont hurt," I said.

Deon agreed and we continued on with dinner. That's why I loved my husband. He was always behind me one hundred percent. He was always willing to help me in any way that he could. That's how a marriage should be, something like a partnership. Where one lacks, the other one picks up the slack and vice versa. When I was out there in the world, I could never imagine myself being married. I always thought that it would be boring, and that you wouldn't have your own life anymore. But that was far from true. To me, marriage enhanced my life. I still had my ace, Rochelle to hang out with. Plus I had the same lover every night, that I knew and trusted. He protected me and our kids with all that was in him, and to me that was the sweetest thing. All that running around that I used to do, I didn't miss it a bit. Now I had stability in my life, and it felt great.

CHAPTER 3: Stepping In

The next morning, I stepped off my flight tired as hell! Once we got back to the hotel after dinner, the kids wanted to go to the pool. Then they wanted to stay up and pillow fight. They didn't conk out until after one a.m. Then I had to pump so that Deon would have milk for Summer when I left. Then he decided he wanted some special time that we had to sneak and do in the shower since the kids were in our room. Once I finally got to bed at around three o'clock, Summer was waking up at around three thirty to nurse. And to top it all off I had to wake up at five so that I could make my flight at six thirty. I was not in the friendliest mood. I picked up my rental car and drove the rest of the way to Aunt Lucinda's house. Once I got there, it was the same as it had always been. Quiet. Low cut grass with daffodils throughout the yard. I had tried so may times to move Aunt Lucinda into a bigger house but she wasn't hearing it. She had worked hard, and had finally paid it off, and she was proud of that. So after a while I got tired of arguing with her, and just let her have her way.

I walked up to the front door and used my key to get in. Aunt Lucy was sitting in the living room on the couch reading her Bible. I smiled. Her morning routine still hadn't changed. She looked up smiled.

"Good morning," she said.
"Good morning," I said back.
"So where is she?" I asked.
"Still in bed sleep."
"Oh OK. Well let me get up there and get her. Our plane leaves at nine thirty."
"OK, her bags are right there," Aunt Lucinda pointed under the dining room table."
"OK."
I walked up the stairs and into Violet's room. It was a damn mess. I wanted to slap the hell out of her just for that. If Mama would have saw her room like this, Violet's behind would have been sore. I walked over to her bed and looked at her. She was

underneath the covers with her mouth wide open. Well it looked like it was time to break her beauty rest.

"Get up," I said shaking her.

"What," she spoke in a sleep induced stupor.

"I said get up. You knew you were supposed to be coming with me and you didn't come home.'"

"Oh my God I'm sleepy!"

"So am I, come on lets go."

"I'm not going I don't have to go with you," Violet said putting her head under her pillow.

At this point I had it. I was tired. I hadn't slept all night. I still had to get back in town and stop past the daycare. Plus we still had to make our one o'clock appointment at the school. I tried to be patient, regardless of the fact that I really wanted to knock her head off.

"I'm only gonna tell you one more time. Get up and get yourself together we have to catch this flight by nine thirty I don't have time to play games with you."

It seemed to me that I had been talking to myself because Violet didn't budge, nor respond. That was it, time to resort to old measures. I ripped the blanket off of her and threw it on the floor. Before she could even attempt to do or say anything I was grabbing her by her ankles and pulling her onto the floor.

"Aunt Lucy! Get her she in here putting her hands on me!" Violet screamed.

Her screams were in vain. Aunt Lucinda didn't come to her rescue. I guess she was really fed up after all.

"Now get up and get your stank ass in the shower. Get yourself together you got thirty minutes," I said.

"I said I'm not going!"

Violet got up from the floor and made a mad dash for the bathroom. She slammed the door and tried to lock it behind her. Unfortunately for her, she didn't move fast enough. I kicked the door and it flew open. I bust in and grabbed her by her hair.

"Now I tried to be nice despite the fact that you didn't deserve it. But now I'm gonna have to show you how mean I can get," I said. "Now since you wanna be dumb Imma treat you like you're dumb. Now you are gonna wear your pajamas and your nappy head just like that to the airport. Lets go."

I led her down the stairs by her hair. She begged and pleaded to stay. I declined.

"Aunt Lucy can you bring her bags to the car for me?" I asked as I dragged Violet out of the front door.

"OK," she said.

After getting Violet in the car, I was exhausted. She was gonna catch hell once we got back to Baltimore. I had no plans on doing all that wrestling with that damn girl. Aunt Lucinda brought the bags to the car.

"OK. I will call you later on tonight. If I messed up the bathroom door just get an estimate and I will give you the money to pay for it," I said preparing to pull off.

"OK. Yall be safe. Violet baby I love you, I'll talk to you later," Aunt Lucinda said.

Violet didn't respond. I looked at her in the rear view mirror. She just sat in the backseat with her arms folded, pouting.

"Don't you hear my aunt talking to you? You better say something!" I demanded.

"Bye," she mumbled.

Aunt Lucy looked at me with so much hurt in her eyes, but at the same time I could tell that she was somewhat relieved.

"She will get over it," I said. "Get some rest."

"OK. Talk to you later," she replied as I drove away.

The ride to the airport was a quiet one. Neither of us said a word. Violet had an attitude, so she called herself giving me the silent treatment. I could care less because the peace and quiet allowed me some space in my mind to map out my day one more time. I had a busy day ahead of me, so I wasn't for no mess. Once we pulled up to the airport I decided that it was time to let her know that I wasn't for no foolishness.

"Now look," I said. "I gotta check this rental car in, then we can go check our bags and stuff. You are going to get out of this car. You are not going to attempt to run away. If you do I will chase you down and embarrass you. I mean what I say. Do you understand what I just said to you?"
"Yes," Violet said.
"Violet I am not playing if you start acting a fool I am really gonna hurt you," I reiterated.
"OK," she said.

So after returning the car and checking our bags, it was time to board our flight. The flight from VA to Baltimore was very short, so in the blink of an eye we were landing. I had parked my car at the airport the day before when the kids and I had flown to Deon's game. It was a good thing that I had done that and not gotten a ride, because I would've had to wait to be picked up and I was pressed for time. Once we got to the house I was in business mode. I showed Violet to her room.
"I have to go past the daycare for a minute. That should give you enough time to eat something, wash your tail and get dressed. I will be back here at twelve. Make sure you are ready to go," I instructed her, then I was out the door.

I got back in the car and headed over to check on my business. I made sure to drop in at least twice a week, just to make sure that I showed my face. Even though I didn't work in the daycare itself, I always wanted to make sure that my employees knew that I wasn't far away. I always wanted to make sure that things were in order. I had to be positive that the children were being cared for properly, that the center was clean and up to par, and that my employees were always working on the correct code of conduct. I arrived at the center and a smile spread across my face. I always felt joy when I was there. To see your business bloom is one of the best feelings in the world. I was thrilled to have had the opportunity to become a business owner.

I walked in and was delighted with what I saw. Happy kids, smiling employees, pretty babies, and clean surroundings.

Yes, this is what I liked to see. I walked into the office area where Shanika sat at her desk.

"Hey there," I greeted her.

"Hey how you doing boss lady?"

"I'm good no complaints. So how's everything going around here? Good I hope."

"Yes mam. Here are all the payments for last week," she handed me the manilla envelope.

"Thank you. So everything came on time?"

"Yeah. Everything was good. All our payments were on time. Well all except one."

"Is this the same one you mentioned to me before?" I asked Shanika.

"Yes. Same one. I know I couldn't think of her name off hand when I mentioned her the last time. But I wrote it down this time. Elaina Baxter."

That name rang in my ears like a bell. Elaina Baxter. Now what was the probability of this? I knew that we were speaking about the same Elaina that was once my best friend. The same Elaina that had betrayed me. I had to tuck my feelings and keep on my professional face.

"OK. Is this a whole payment or-"

"No. A copay. She receives child care vouchers. The reason why her account has raised my eyebrow is because it has been late seven times now. Also, the attendance of her children isn't good either," Shanika stated.

"Really?" I asked. "How many children does she have enrolled?"

"Four"

"Ages?"

"Um let me see," Shanika looked down at the paper work. "Three months, two, three, and five."

"OK. Wow. So the five year old is in the kindergarten class right?" I asked.

"Yes. But she is behind in all her assignments. Her attendance is really hurting her. Either she is late, or she is absent."

My business was still fairly new not even two years old, so this type of situation was new to me. My center had children up to the age of five. The youngest we took were six weeks old. Our pre-k and kindergarten classes were regulated on Baltimore city public school's standards, so attendance was important. On a personal level I knew that children with attendance issues also had issues at home. I wondered what was going on in Elaina's home. I wondered what made her come to Baltimore. And as if timing wasn't right enough, right in the middle of my conversation about Elaina, she walked into the center with her children.
"Well it looks like we spoke her up," Shanika said.
"OK. I will go talk to her," I said.
"OK. Good luck," Shanika replied.

I walked up to Elaina and all the memories flooded my brain like a tidal wave. How I loved her like a sister, and how we did everything together. Then how she stabbed me in the back. I always thought that if I saw her again that I would lash out and attack, but at this moment I didn't feel any of that. Years had passed and I was truly in a better place. Franko was long gone, and there was nothing I could do to change that, or the fact that he had stepped out on me with my best friend. I had finally gotten over it. But she didn't look like the same Elaina. Yes she was a woman now, but she looked beat down. The world had been getting the best of her and it showed. There were dark circles around her eyes and she was unusually thin. Her posture wasn't even good. I looked at her and I felt bad for her. No, I could no longer be mad at her, I felt for her. But I guess Elaina hadn't gotten over me whipping her tail yet, because as soon as she saw me walking in her direction her stance became rigid. I couldn't blame her though, since I had told her that every time I saw her I was gonna whip her ass. Still I continued to walk over to her cool, calm, and collected.
"Hello Ms. Baxter," I greeted her in the most professional tone that I could.
She looked me up and down. "What?" she asked as if she hadn't heard me.

"I said hello," I responded still trying to remain professional.
"Yeah whatever. Don't speak to me," she said taking the baby bag off of her shoulder before she sat it on the floor.
I shook it off. "Well I don't want to take up too much of your time, but I need to speak to you about your late copay and your children's attendance."
"Is there a reason why you all in my business?" she asked heavily salted.
"Why, I thought you'd never ask," I said sarcastically. "I am the owner of this fine establishment that you have chosen to enroll your children into. If I am not mistaken, before your children started here there was a contract that you signed. Correct?"

Elaina looked at me like I was the scum of the earth. I could tell that hearing that I was actually the owner of a well established business did not sit well with her. As well as the fact the position that I held gave me the upper hand in a situation that she was involved in didn't brighten her day either. She just stood there looking at me not saying a word.
"In that contract it specifically states that you are responsible for the payment of any fees that you owe on time. In the event that this does not happen, your children are subject to being removed from our enrollment list. Poor attendance also carries that same consequence. Now I would never want to do that, because obviously you have things to do. I am assuming that is why you have your children in child care. But at the same time I am running a business, so I have to stand my ground on the rules that I have set forth."

Elaina looked at me with so much hatred in her eyes. Her lip turned up as if she she were disgusted. So I decided to take the professional tone down a few notches so that I could get on her level for a second.
"Is it a reason why you're looking at me with the screw face?" I asked Elaina.
"Yea. I don't want my kids coming here that's why," Elaina said.
"Well then don't let your kids come here. I don't know why you're mad at me anyway. You crossed me, not the other way

around. I don't owe you a thing sweet heart. But any who as you can see I'm not hurting for business around here so by all means, if you don't want your kids here then take them out."

Elaina took a deep breath, then turned around and walked out. I watched her walk down the street through the glass doors, and shook my head. I went back into Shanika's office and let her know that if Elaina was late with her payment again, then her children would have to be taken off of our enrollment list. After all, business was just that. Business. I left the daycare and made my way back home so that I could take Violet up to the school for our tour. The whole ride home I couldn't help but to think about the look on Elaina's face when I told her that I was the owner. There was a life lesson in that situation. Be careful who you cross, because you never know when or where your paths with the person you did wrong will cross.

I parked in front of my house and took a deep breath. I really had no idea that Elaina's kids were enrolled in my daycare center. I still hadn't processed it all. Wow. Life has a tendency to throw you curve balls. I definitely didn't see that one coming. I had to clear my mind now though, it was time for me to switch gears. Just a few moments ago I wore the hat of a business owner, now I had to flip to guardian and care giver. I beeped the horn. Violet came walking out of the house and got into the car. Again it was another silent car ride. I still wasn't concerned though. I knew that she would get used to be in Baltimore after she realized that no matter how much she pouted, I wasn't budging. She was here to stay. Well at least until she was an adult, then she would be free to make her own decisions.

We pulled up to the school, and I was pleased just by looking at the outside. It looked even better than it did on the website in person. The lawn was well manicured, and the windows were clean and bright. Once we got inside, the positive feelings that I had about the school had elevated. Everyone was so friendly, and the halls were quiet. Yes this is exactly what Violet needed, decency and order. After entering the main office I was sold. I was absolutely sure that this was the right school for my sister.

    Finally we sat with Mrs. Dulaney the head mistress, or what we call principals in public schools. She began by telling me the school's mission statement. "Building scholars for life, leading our youth to the light." she went on with the curriculum and daily schedule. I looked over at Violet and her expression showed that she was uninterested. I figured that much because if it was up to her, she would be in VA hooking school doing God knows what with God knows who. I had no qualms about being he reason that all that foolishness had come to an end. No qualms at all.

    After speaking with Mrs. Dulaney we were taken on a tour by Mrs. Latowsky, the head of admissions. Violet dragged her feet full of gloom and doom, and my mood remained chipper and upbeat as we were shown around. We looked into a classroom, where the students were testing. Everyone was sitting so nicely, with their neatly pressed uniforms. I couldn't wait for Violet to put her uniform on and come to school. Violet finally spoke.

"So what's this an all girl class or something?"

"This is an all girl school," Mrs. Latowsky answered.

    Violet's face broke down as if she smelled something foul. How dare I try to enroll her in an all girl school? She was heated with me. After the tour was over, I was ready to seal the deal. We were lead to the finance office where I signed all the necessary paper work, and turned in all the necessary information that was needed for Violet to start.

"Why don't you head on over to the uniform department and get fitted while your mom gets everything squared away over here," Ms. Nelson, the director of finance said to Violet.

"She is not my mother, she is my sister," Violet said as she stomped out of the room.

"Well somebody isn't in the best of moods today," Ms. Nelson joked with me.

"Yeah I know, but this is good for her. I just brought her up here from Virginia, so she is still missing her old surroundings. She'll get over it," I responded.

"She is very blessed to have you as a sister. It's not too often where I see young people who see the need to make an investment into education."

"Thanks. But I'm just trying to give her all the things that I never had. I want to give her a fair chance to succeed. My mother didn't have the financial capabilities to send me to a school like this. Now that I am in the position to make these type of decisions I don't take it lightly. I want my sister to be successful, and it all starts with education."

"You are so right," Ms. Nelson replied.

After writing a check for Violet's first three months of tuition, her uniforms, and her text books, we were all set. I thanked everyone for being so helpful then Violet and I headed to the car. I was ecstatic that Violet would be starting school the next day. Now I could go home, unwind, and wait for Deon to call me from the airport once he and the kids had landed. At least I could get a few snoozes in because I was exhausted. Violet sat in the passenger seat with her arms folded. Every so often she would huff and puff, which was starting to get under my skin. Finally I had enough of her b.s.

"What the hell is your problem?" I asked her.

"I want to go home," she said.

"Newsflash honey. This is your home now," I said pulling into my garage.

"No it's not."

"Violet let me tell you something. I am not Aunt Lucy. You might've got away with all that smart mouth stuff with her, but it ain't gon' fly with me. I am the adult, you are the child."

"I'm not a child I'm a teenager."

"OK and in the real world that means you are a child. You don't know shit. Nothing at all. You don't have the means to take care of yourself. Like I said, you are a child," I informed her.

"I hate that school," was her next complaint.

"Well you better learn to love it because that is where you are gonna be until you graduate."

"It ain't even no boys there! What I want to be sitting around a bunch of girls for? Even all of the teachers are girls! That school is just dumb I just want to go back to my old life! That school is too strict!"

"If you are in school, what do you need to see a boy for? That's what got you into the situation you're in now. Boys. All you think about is boys. They got your mind polluted Violet. You need to focus on your education. Them boys ain't going nowhere. They ain't gonna do nothing but bring you trouble and heartache. I'm telling you what I know Violet you better listen," I tried to school her.

"Yeah says the person that had a baby in the tenth grade," she said reaching for the door handle. I quickly hit the child lock button.

"What did you say to me?"

"I'm just saying you doing all this preaching but you had a baby in the tenth grade. At least I don't have no baby."

"Yes I did have a baby young. Matter of fact I was dumb enough to have two. But that is what gives me all the more wisdom to know which way I don't want yo to go. I know where being out there will get you. I have done it all. So I can truly say that I am speaking from experience. That is something that you don't have. You are a little girl thinking with your vagina and that ain't gon' get you far. At this point in your life you don't even know your own body. You don't even know what's good and what's not, so you need to slow down. All you're gonna wind up doing is getting pregnant, catching something that you can't get rid of, and you're gonna make a name for yourself. Trust me you don't want that. Now you are here with me and that's how it's gonna be. You will go to school and you will come home. You will do what you are told. You will not be in the streets acting a fool. You will have a curfew. You will have chores. As long as you follow my rules we will get along fine. If you don't you will see how I really get down. Got it?"

"Yes," Violet said with tears streaming down her face.
	I hit the child lock button and Violet got out of the car. She stormed into the house and into her room. I sat down on the sofa.
"Lord what have I gotten myself into?" I asked God.

CHAPTER 4: Trust

I scrolled through the contacts until I saw a name that stuck out like a sore thumb. Tiffany. Hmmmm... Now who could this be? I flipped through my mental Rolodex. I couldn't think of any close family members with that name. Certainly no friends either. Any female friends I had to know about, that was our agreement. And if it wasn't for the sake of business I didn't play the new friends game. My blood boiled, I thought that we were better than this. I wanted to hold it in and do a bit of investigating, but I really didn't feel like it. I was going to take it straight to the source.
"Deon!" I yelled.
"Huh?"
"So who is Tiffany?" I asked him.
"Who?" he asked in a sleepy fog.
"So what you an owl now nigga don't play with me I will bust you upside your head with this remote."
"I don't know what you're talking about Rosie," Deon said, rubbing his eyes.
"Listen. I don't have time for the games Deon. We are supposed to be married. So all these little groupie hoes that keep sniffing around you, you better get them in check. Keep it up and see if you won't be by yourself," I said, pulling his cell phone out of my pocket.
"What do you have my phone for?" Deon asked.
"Because you have a tendency of carrying it around everywhere with you, and I wanted to know what was so important about this phone that you carry it around more than you carry Summer."
"Come on now Rosie don't start the crazy stuff. I can't believe you would go through my phone while I was sleep," he whined.
"Well I can't believe that you would tell me you love me, ask me to marry you, and then want to play these childish games," I responded, throwing the phone at him.

Deon caught the phone, which made me even more furious. I was trying to hit him upside his head with it but the football player in him made him catch the damn phone. God he made me sick. He entered the password into the phone and then began scrolling through it.

"Are you talking about this 443 number?" he finally asked.

"I don't know. Whatever number that is under the name Tiffany. What I look like memorizing the number?"

"The same way you look cracking my password and going through my phone while I was sleep."

"You act like the password was that hard to figure out. It's Deonte's birthday dummy... How hard is that to guess?"

"It don't matter you still shouldn't be going through my phone."

"Whatever Deon don't be putting up smoke screens. Who the hell is Tiffany?" I asked again.

"It's some girl's number that Levelle saved in my phone when we were at lunch the other day," he said.

"Now do you really expect me to believe that?" I asked him.

"Yea because you asked me a question and I gave you an answer what else do you want me to say Rose?"

"Why didn't he save the number in his own phone? Wait a minute ain't he married?"

"He left his phone in the car... And yeah he is married, but that ain't none of my business Rose," Deon responded.

"So that's the type of dudes you choose to associate with? The type that like to cheat on their wives? Birds of a feather flock together," I remarked.

"What happened to trusting your mate Rose?"

"What ever happened to you giving me something to trust with your sneaky ass? Because I don't believe this dumb ass story you telling!"

"Girl go ahead somewhere," Deon said before he rolled over and went back to sleep.

  Wow, I was trying to have a serious conversation with my husband about a serious matter and he went to sleep while I was talking. How mature. I started to pour a bucket of cold water on him, but I realized that would be doing more harm than help. I went and got my pen and pad and began to write. What do you do,

when your past hurts cause you to constantly accuse?
How to yourself do you prove,
that everyone's motive isn't to use you?
When does the pain go away?
Can you ever truly trust?
Do you really love or is that just what you say?
To this new found love will you ever adjust?
Are they really about what they portray?
I would give my all for him to see,
all the insecurities inside my mind.
To make all his desires to be of me,
and realize that there is no love like mine.
What must I do to flip the switch,
and brighten his prospective?
That in order to scratch this itch,
honesty and unity must be his main objective?
No love is not blind,
we just choose to see what we want.
Yes if you seek you shall find,
so stop making me feel like finding is what I want.
This love doesn't have to be complicated,
it can be as sweet as pie.
Just as long as this love is reciprocated,
and you don't shame me with a lie.

CHAPTER 5: Baby Deon

"Mommy!" Miracle yelled upstairs.
"Yea!" I yelled back to her.
"Mommy come here!" she yelled again.
"No you come here," I answered back.

     I sat on my bed Indian style, deeply engrossed in my Bible. It read:
Proverbs 31
10 Who can find a virtuous woman? For her price is far above rubies.
11 The heart of her husband doth safely trust in her, so that he shall have no need of spoil.
12 She will do him good and not evil all the days of her life.
13 She seeketh wool and flax, and worketh willingly with her hands.
14 She is like the merchant's ships: She bringeth her food from afar.
15 She riseth also while it is night, and giveth meat to her household, and a portion to her maidens.
16 She considereth a field and buyeth it: with the fruit of her hands she planteth a vineyard.
17 She girdeth her loins with strength and strengtheneth her arms.
18 She percieveth that her merchandise is good: her candle goeth not out by night.
19 She layeth her hands to the spindle, and her hands to the distaff.
20 She stretcheth her hand to the poor: yea, she reacheth forth her hands to the needy.
21 She is not afraid of the snow for her household. For all her household are clothed with scarlet.
22 She maketh herself coverings of tapestry; her clothing is of silk and purple.
23 Her husband is known in the gates, when sitting among the elders of the land.
24 She maketh fine linen and selleth it: and delivereth girdles unto the merchant.

25 Strength and honour are her clothing; and she shall rejoice in time to come.
26 She openeth her mouth with wisdom; and in her tongue is the law of kindness.
27 She looketh well to the ways of her house. Hold and eateth not the bread of idleness.
28 Her children arise up, and call her blessed; her husband also, and he praiseth her.
29 Many daughters have done virtuously, but thou excellest them all.
30 Favour is deceitful, and beauty is vain: but a woman that feareth the LORD, she shall be praised.
31 Give her of the fruit of her hands: and let her own works praise her in the gates.
"Wow," I thought. "I have a long way to go, but at least I'm on the right track."

I heard the sound of footsteps coming down the hall. I was curious to know what had Miracle yelling from downstairs like that. She knew that it got under my skin when someone tried to talk to me from another room. She must've wanted something. Miracle peeped her head into my doorway.
"Mommy," she said again.
"Yes Miracle. Wassup?"

I couldn't help but to hear whining. I knew it wasn't Miracle because she was standing right in front of my face, and I knew it wasn't Summer because she was napping.
"What is that noise?" I asked.
"Him," Miracle said stepping into my room.

Miracle was holding the hand of a little boy. A toddler to be exact. I was completely confused.
"Whose baby do you have?" I asked her.
"I don't know," she responded.
"What do you mean you don't know? Where did he come from?"
"A lady."
"Miracle don't make me get mad. Please tell me what is going on!"

Tears welled up in Miracle's eyes. "Mommy I don't know. I was downstairs watching TV. then I heard somebody knocking on the door. I opened it and this lady was standing there with him. She said give him to his daddy and pushed him in the house," she said before she burst into tears.
"It's okay," I said. "I didn't mean to yell at you. I just wanted to know what was going on that's all. I'm not mad at you. OK? And I told you before that you are not supposed to answer the door. If you hear somebody knocking, you come get me OK?"
"Okay," Miracle sniffled.

It had slipped my mind how sensitive Miracle was. At times I had trouble believing that she belonged to me. How could a hard ass like me had given birth to a child that would cry if you said "boo" to her? Any who, I had to ponder on that later. There was a more important matter at hand. I had someone's child standing in my bedroom, and I had no idea who he was. I got up from the bed and walked over to him.
"Hi handsome, what's your name? Can you tell me your name?"
"Deon," he said rubbing his eyes.

I wasn't sure that I had heard him correctly, so I asked him again.
"What's your name?"
"Deon," he whined looking at the floor.

My stomach dropped to the floor. I couldn't believe what I was hearing. I gently lifted his chin and looked at his face. The resemblance was uncanny. Yup. His name was Deon alright. I was so mad you could've fried an egg on my head. But I managed to keep my composure. I picked him up and he wrapped his arms around my neck. This poor baby had been through some things, I could feel it.
"What's your Mommy's name?" I asked him.
"Mommy," he said.

I already figured that he wouldn't be able to tell me that. He was no older than three. I was enraged. What type of woman would leave her child with another child? She didn't even know if there was an adult in the house or not! My head pounded. In the middle of my thoughts, the little boy spoke. "I'm hungry," he said.

Tears welled up in my eyes. Not only did she drop this precious child on my doorstep, but she didn't even have the decency to feed him before she brought him. I blinked the tears away. I couldn't let Miracle see me cry. I had to be strong. I had to take control of the situation.
"Miracle watch TV. up here and listen out for the baby for me. If she wakes up come get me. I'm going downstairs to fix him something to eat."
"OK," she replied.

Miracle climbed up onto my bed and reached for the remote. I took the little boy downstairs to the kitchen. I had no idea what he liked or if he had any food allergies. I decided to warm him up a plate of leftovers from dinner from the night before. Once the plate had finished warming in the microwave, I sat him in Summer's high chair. I put his hands together and said grace. He smiled at me and my heart melted. It was hard to stay upset when I had such a handsome little boy smiling in my face. I began to feed him some rice and gravy, and some broccoli.
"Um good," his little voice said.
I laughed, "oh so you like my cooking?"

He nodded his head yes and I laughed again. This little boy was something else. I still wanted to call Deon and rip him a new one, but I knew he wouldn't answer because he was at practice. He always called right after he was done, so I would deal with him then. I fed my new friend until the plate was completely clean. Once he saw that the food was gone, he started crying.
"What's wrong?" I asked him.
"Hungry," he cried.
"You want more?"

He nodded his head yes. My heart shattered into a million pieces. I felt so bad. When was the last time this boy had eaten? I still couldn't believe what was going on. This was

beyond crazy. I fixed him a second plate and he was satisfied after he finished it. I pulled out one of Lil Franko's cups with the crazy straw attached to it.
"Ooooh," Baby Deon said.

I laughed. He was such a bright little boy. He was so full of personality. I handed him the cup and he sucked the juice down.
"Wet," he said after he finished drinking.
"Yea, I know juice is wet," I said.

I picked him up, ready to take him back upstairs. I felt wetness on my arm. Then it hit me. He was trying to tell me that he was wet! I shook my head. He was soaked! I was pissed! Not only did his sorry ass excuse for a mother just drop him off unannounced, he was starving and she didn't change him either! I knew for a fact that he didn't soak through his pamper within the thirty minutes that he had been in my care. I took him to my room and stripped him down. I was disgusted when I took off his pamper. He had the most terrible diaper rash that I had ever seen. Again my blood started to boil.
"Get it together Rose," I said aloud.
"You OK Mommy?" Miracle asked me, taking her focus away from the TV. for a split second.
"Yes I'm fine love bug," I said to her.

I shook my head and got back focused.
"Imma hook him up," I thought.

I put him in the bath and put some toys in with him so he could play. I sat on the edge of the tub attempting to figure everything out in my head. But it was no use. I couldn't make any type of sense out of this situation. Just then, my phone rang. It was Deon. I took a deep breath then answered.
"Hello," I said.
"Hey babe. What you doing?" he asked.
"Is there something you need to tell me?" I asked disregarding his question.
"No, what you talking 'bout?"

"Deon Imma ask you one more time. Is there anything that you need to tell me?" I asked again, trying to give him a chance to come clean.

"No… What's going on?" he asked.

"OK so you asked me what I was doing. I'm giving your son a bath."

"Why? Deonte' is old enough to take a bath by his self. What Trina dropped him off? She wasn't supposed to drop him off until Tuesday after he got out of school," Deon said totally oblivious to what was going on.

"No not Deonte'. Your son Deon."

"Deonte' is my son."

"No you idiot! Your other son!"

"I don't have another son."

"Yes you do!" I screamed.

"Hold up. What are you talking about? What's going on?" Deon asked.

"Some random bitch popped up on this doorstep and knocked on the door with your son. Miracle answered the door. She gave him to Miracle and left.

"So how you figure that's my son? And how you gon' take a child not even knowing who he is?"Deon inquired.

"First of all calm your tone. I didn't even hear the door. I was in my room studying my word and Miracle brought him upstairs," I explained.

"OK so I'm still not getting how you figure that's my son," Deon interrupted.

"If you would shut up then I will tell you!"

"Stop screaming!"

"Look anyway she told Miracle to take him to his daddy. I asked him what his name was and he said Deon," I finally finished.

"For real?" Was all Deon could manage to say.

"No for fake. Yes for real do I sound like I'm fucking joking?" I asked.

Baby Deon looked up at me. I had to pull myself together. I couldn't be talking like that around him. I was dead wrong and I knew it.

"I'm sorry baby I didn't mean to say that," I said to him.

"It's cool," Deon said.

"I'm not talking to you I'm talking to the baby."

"Oh."

"OK… So what's going on Deon? Clearly something is going on and I want to know now," I demanded.

"I don't know what's going on your guess is as good as mine," Deon replied.

"Really? So you're really gonna play the dumb role now?"

"I mean what do you want me to say Rose? You don't even know if that's my son or not."

"What do I want you to say? Are you being for real right now? I want you to be honest, that's what I want. I'm not going to sit here and tell you what to say and I don't care what you are talking about because he is your son," I said.

"How do you know? She could be lying," Deon stated.

"He looks just like you Deon. That's how I know," I replied back.

"That is not how you establish paternity Rose," Deon said.

"No shit Sherlock! I know that. I'm just being real. Looking in his face is like staring directly into yours. You cannot deny this boy, you can't."

"That's crazy," Deon said.

"So who is his mother?" I asked.

"Rose can we just talk about this when I get home?"

"No we cannot I want to talk about it now don't try to brush me off. I want answers and I want them now."

"Oh my God," he said.

"Don't use the Lord's name in vain. And um hello I asked you a question. Who is his mother?"

"Rose I don't even know if that's my son."

"He is your son now answer my question."

Deon took a deep breath then he spoke, " Mocha."

"Mocha," I repeated.

"Yea," he confirmed.
"This has got to be a joke you gotta be joking right now."
"Naw," he said.
"So all that talk about it was only me, you only tricked off with me, that's not you, that's not something you would do with everybody, that was just you blowing smoke up my ass right?"
"No Rose. Listen. Just let me explain," he pleaded.
"Oh now you wanna explain? I'm over this whole situation. Come home now and get your son. I'm taking my kids and I'm leaving," I said before I hung up on him.

Tears streamed down my face. I knew that Deon was too good to be true. I felt so stupid. Deon called my phone back to back at least twenty times but I wouldn't answer. I finished bathing Baby Deon, then took him back to my room. Miracle was still watching TV and the baby was still napping. Good thing she was a big baby, because I don't know what I would have put on Baby Deon's butt if she wasn't. I powdered and lotioned him down, then put one of Summer's diapers on him.
"Franko," I called out to my son.
"Yes Ma," he answered back.
"Come here baby," I said.
"OK, here I come. Yea Ma," he said once he got to my room.
"Go in your closet and look in that pile of clothes that I have folded up in there. You know what I'm talking about?"
"No."
"Franko… Remember the clothes that I told you I was donating to the Purple Heart because they were too small for you? Remember?"
"Oh yeah."
"That's the pile I'm talking about. Get a t-shirt from out of there and bring it here for me," I said.
"OK. Who's that?" Franko pointed to Baby Deon.
"This is your step brother."
"But I thought Deonte' was our step brother," Miracle cut in.
"He is. But he is too."
"What's his name?" Franko probed.
"Deon," I answered.

"How old is he?"
"I don't know Lil' Franko just go get me the t-shirt and chill out with all the questions for right now," I said.
"OK," he said before he left the room.
   I bounced baby Deon on my lap until Franko brought the t-shirt to me. I put it on Baby Deon. I couldn't believe what was happening.
"Franko," I called out to him again.
"He peeped his head in the doorway, "Yes."
"What are you in there doing?" I asked.
"Playing my game," he answered.
"Well come get him and take him in the room with you."
"Ma….." Franko whined.
"That's not a request," I replied.
   Lil' Franko dragged his feet back into my room. He ain't like nobody bothering him while he was playing his video games. He was a true game hawk.
"Here take him," I said. "Teach him how to play. He is really smart. I think he will catch on fast."
"OK," Lil' Franko said unenthusiastically.
   After Lil' Franko took Baby Deon off my hands, I grabbed my phone and went to my car. I needed to talk to my bestie. She always gave the best advice. I prayed that she would answer the phone. I knew that she would probably still be tied up teaching her class. Yes, you read it right, her class. Once Deon and I made it official, not only did he give me the money to open up my daycare center, but he had also given her the money to fulfill her life long dream. My girl finally had her own dance studio. She taught dance classes for young girls, who lived in low income households. I was so proud of her. She deserved it.
   So anyway, I got in my car and dialed her number. I needed to be able to talk with no filter. I didn't need any kids eavesdropping on my conversation.
Hey girlie," Rochelle answered.
"Bitch wait 'til I tell you this!" I yelled into the phone.

"Oh my goodness. Hold up. Before you start let me call you back in five minutes. Let me dismiss these girls and Imma call you right back."
"Make sure you call me right back it's really important."
"OK."

    I sat in my garage in my car waiting patiently for her to return my call. This news was burning a hole in my heart. It seemed like forever waiting for Rochelle to call me back. Finally, the phone rang.
"I'm leaving Deon," I said after I slid my finger across the screen.
"What?" Rochelle asked.
"Yes I'm leaving. He ain't all that he is cracked up to be."
"Wait hold on. Calm down. What happened now?"
"Girl I was upstairs reading my Bible. Miracle started yelling my name. I told her to come upstairs, and she came walking in my room with a little boy. I asked her who he was and she told me she didn't know," I began.
"What?" Rochelle interrupted.
"Hold up let me finish telling you. So you know me I'm ready to zap because she brought somebody's baby in my room and couldn't tell me who he was."
"Um hum."
"So finally she tells me that some bitch came knocking on my door, and when she opened it the damn dummy pushed the little boy on her talking 'bout give him to his daddy."
"What?"
"Right. So you know I'm confused as hell. I asked the little boy his name and he said Deon just as clear."
"You lying!"
"No girl I wish I was!"
"Oh my goodness."
"So hold up it gets deeper than that. First of all the baby was starving. He ate two plates. He was dirty and she dropped him off with a wet diaper. I go to give him a bath and take his diaper off, and he got the nastiest rash that I have ever seen! Girl I liked to die!"

"Damn that's messed up."
"Yes! But hold up, this is he kicker. So Deon finally called me after he finished practice. So I'm telling this idiot what happened, and all he can say is how do I know that's his son. I'm like the little boy is your twin! You can't deny him! So he was still denying it and acting dumb. I was tired of the bullshit and just came flat out and asked him who his mother is. Guess who it is?" I said.
"Um I don't know. Trina?" Rochelle guessed.
"Nope. I wish she was. Guess again."
"Girl I don't know just give me the tea!"
"Mocha," I blurted out.
"Mocha who?" Rochelle asked.
"Mocha Mocha. Mocha from the club Mocha."
"Ugly ass Mocha?"
"Yes that duck face whore," I said.
"What? How in the hell did that happen?" Rochelle asked.
"Girl I don' know. I told him to come home and get his damn son cuz I'm packing my kids up and I'm blowing this joint."
"So you don't want to know what happened at least?" Rochelle probed.
"Hell no! For what? What it all boils down to is he got a baby that don't belong to me. That little boy ain't no older than three years old."
"Wow. Where he at now?"
"Who?"
"The baby."
"In the room with Lil' Franko playing the game."
"Damn I know he mad," Rochelle laughed.
"And you know it. You know he likes to be alone with his game," I laughed.
"Right."
"And look. Why Miracle talking 'bout she thought Deonte' was her step brother," I continued to laugh.
"Shid, Miracle wanna know what the hell is going on," Rochelle cracked up.
I let out a sigh, "I'm laughing but ain't a damn thing funny."

"It's gonna be OK. I'm not gonna tell you what to do in your marriage because I really don't have a clue. I've never been married. I just think you should find out what happened because it's a lot of unanswered questions," Rochelle suggested.

"I don't know Ro. The way I'm feeling I might just punch him in the mouth."

"Girl cut it out. Just hear the man out."

"I might. But let me get in this house girl. Summer should be getting up from her nap soon and I guess I should be starting dinner. Let me text this dummy and tell him to bring some pampers or pull ups or something in here for his child. Because you know that girl ain't drop him off here with nothing."

"Oh she really went hard," Rochelle said.

"Yup, he got on one of Summer's pampers," I said.

"Girl you got your work cut out for you now."

"Yeah so for his sake he better hope that I give this forgiveness thing a shot. That's what my pastor preached about last Sunday," I recalled.

"Well that's a start. Give it a try Ms. Zap Out Queen," Rochelle joked.

"You wouldn't have zapped out if it was you?" I asked.

"Hell yeah," Rochelle laughed.

"Girl you crazy," I laughed. "Bye."

"Bye."

My convo with Rochelle calmed me down a little bit. I wasn't as angry as I was before, but I still was angry though. It was so crazy because around this time last year everything was so beautiful. Things were going so smooth in my life. I had gotten married, had a new baby, and opened up a new business. But here came a storm cloud rising, just when I had gotten used to good things happening.

I took a deep breath, then took my behind back in the house. I went in the kitchen and looked around in the refrigerator; I needed to start dinner. I looked at the chicken that I had been defrosting and suddenly realized that I didn't feel up to cooking. I picked up the phone and called Deon's assistant, and asked her to bring Chinese over for dinner. We tried to avoid having strangers coming to the house, since Deon was a football player and had a lot of crazed fans. We didn't need them or any reporters popping up. That's why I couldn't understand how Mocha knew where we lived. That was going to be another question that I needed to ask Deon. After I spoke with his assistant, I texted him telling him to bring his son some diapers.

    The rest of the day was OK. I chilled with the kids and relaxed. I did a couple of loads of laundry too. I kept checking the time as it got later and later. Deon still wasn't home and I was growing impatient. I needed answers and it was taking too long for me to get them. Before I knew it bedtime had crept up for the kids. I got them bathed and put them to bed. Then it dawned on me. Violet wasn't home yet. Where in the world was this girl? I picked up the phone and called Rochelle. Maybe she could help me get some kind of location on my sister.
"Hey girlie wassup?" Rochelle answered.
"Hey Ro. I was just wondering did you see somebody picking Violet up from class today? Or did she leave by herself?" I asked.
"Oh Rosie that totally slipped my mind since you were talking to me about what happened earlier. Violet didn't even show up for class today," Rochelle stated.
"Really?"
"Nope. I meant to ask you why but like I said I got so wrapped up in our conversation, it slipped my mind."
    I let out a deep sigh.
"Is something wrong?" Rochelle asked.
"Yeah. I haven't seen or heard from her all day. She still ain't home and her phone is going straight to voice mail," I replied.
"Oh goodness. Well you think you should call the police?"
"No. I just have that gut feeling that she is with that clown ass little boy. Plus she gotta be gone at least twenty four hours to file a missing person report."
"OK. So what you gonna do?"

"I don't know. Like I said I got a sneaky suspicion she is with that funny looking boy. I can't stand his ass," I said.
"Well you already know the more you hate him, the more she is gonna love him. I went through the same thing with Laila," Rochelle responded.
"Girl I know. I hope I didn't bite off more than I can chew. It's times like these when I really wish that my mother was alive."
"I know. But you are strong. Your aunt needed help with her and you stepped in. A lot of sisters wouldn't have took on that responsibility. You go it. It ain't gon' be easy. They get that little tingle between their legs and they go loco," Rochelle laughed.
"Yeah, I know," I laughed.
"So did you talk to Deon?" Rochelle changed the subject.
"Nope. Girl he ain't even bring his box head ass in here yet," I replied.
"Well damn, where he at?"
"I don't have a clue," I answered back.
　　　Just then I saw lights shining coming up the drive way to the garage. I already knew who it was.
"Speaking of the devil," I said. "He just pulled up. Imma call you in the morning and let you know what happened.
"Ard bye."
　　　I took another deep breath. I couldn't shake this uneasy feeling. I knew I was about to get some information that was going to piss me off. So I sat at the dining room table and waited for Deon to come in the house.
"So where you been?" I asked as soon as he was in my eyes view.
"Just trying to clear my head," Deon responded.
"You sure you weren't at a hotel somewhere making another baby?"
"This is why I didn't wanna come home. I knew you were gonna be on this type of shit."
"I mean do you blame me?"
"No but you are blaming me though."
"Yes I am! Why wouldn't I? Ain't you the one who had sex with the damn girl? What the hell is wrong with you? Am I

crazy or something? Because it seems to me that it is definitely your fault!"

"Yeah it is! But can you just let me explain?"

I was about ready to punch his lights out. He had definitely lost his scruples. But I just had to hear his so called explanation.

"I'm listening," I said.

"It happened the night you told me you were back at the club. I was mad and I wasn't thinking straight. I wanted to get back at you for lying to me. I was drinking and I called the club and I asked for her. So we agreed to meet up later that night and we did. It was only one night."

"That's all it takes when you don't strap up dummy."

"Look Rose damn! You don' gotta keep rubbing it in my face!"

"Don't yell at me you're the one who did the dumb shit not me! So you meaning to tell me all this time you never knew that she was pregnant, or that she had the baby? That seems crazy to me," I said.

"Well.. One time she did come to the training camp. She just popped up taking about she was pregnant. I ain't believe her though. I got security to escort her off the premises."

"You got her escorted off the premises because she came to tell you that she was pregnant. Wow you're really a stand up guy."

"No, she was acting crazy Rose. She was talking about how much she loved me and wanted to be with me and we have to raise our family together. Just screaming and hollering talking about she was going to kill herself if I wasn't with her. So I didn't believe her because I thought she was just trying to get my attention. I couldn't have her doing that at my job Rose you know that."

"And you decided to keep this from me because?"

"Honestly I thought she was just trying to get me to be with her because of my money. I really didn't think that she was pregnant," Deon rationalized.

"OK but what if she saw me in the street somewhere and approached me about it? You know word gets around fast so

I'm pretty sure somebody told her that we were together," I said.
"I didn't even think that far Rose. I really didn't. And listen, I don't want you to leave me. I love you. I want this marriage to work. You mean the world to me. You are my wife and you gave me a beautiful daughter. And I love Lil' Franko and Miracle like they are my own. I realize now that I should've told you about the whole thing and I am sorry. But it was a one time thing between me and her and it was before we even made it official." Deon got on his knees and wrapped his arms around my legs, "Baby please don't leave me."

    I was still pissed so I was trying to think of something mean to say to him, but I couldn't think of anything. For the first time in a long time, I was speechless. He was right after all, he had laid down with that beast before we were an item, so I couldn't hold something against him that was before me. It looked like I was going to be sticking it out after all.

"You are so lucky that I love you," I said finally.
"Not lucky, blessed. Ain't that what you always say?"

    Deon stood up and embraced me tightly. He looked me in my eyes, and we kissed passionately.
"I love you," he said
"I love you too," I cooed.
"So where is he?" Deon asked me.
"In our bed with the rest of the kids," I replied.
"Well let me go up there and see him," Deon said.

    Once we got in the room Deon approached the bed. I stood back so that I could see his reaction. He looked at Baby Deon, then he looked back at me. His eyes were glassy. At that moment, I knew that he knew for himself that was his son.
"He looks just like Deonte' when he was little, " he finally spoke.
"I told you he is your twin. Couldn't deny him if you tried," I said.
"Yeah, you're right. Damn I have another son. It's OK. Imma make this situation right. I missed too much of his life already."

"Ask God to forgive you and move on babe. That's all you can do."
"What type of mother could just leave their child like that?"
"I don't know Deon. But I didn't even tell you everything. When he got here he was starving. He ate two big plates of dinner from the other night. He was wet. His clothes were filthy and he has a diaper rash that is out of this world. Plus she didn't send any clothes or anything else with him either."
"What? I'm gonna get this whole thing straightened out. I'm calling my lawyer in the morning. I'm keeping my son. That shit is just ridiculous. She is so trifling I seriously doubt that she is even gonna come back for him. But if she does I ain't letting him go."
"Well I'm behind you one hundred percent," I told him.
"Thanks babe. Well I guess I will have to call Miley in the morning and get her to go get him some clothes and stuff."
"Sounds like a plan," I said cheerfully.
"I'm tired," Deon yawned. "Come get in the shower with me so we can get in the bed. That's if we can find a spot."
"I wish I could. But I gotta sit up and wait for Violet to get in here. I can't get comfortable until I know that she is here, and that she is OK," I said.
"Oh damn she ain't here yet? I thought she was in her room sleep. It's almost two thirty," Deon replied.
"Naw she still out being hot in the ass. But Imma fix her when she comes in here."
"Don't beat her up too bad," Deon chuckled.
"Oh no I'm not. I just gotta show her who's the boss that's all," I said.

So I went and sat in the living room on the sofa, watching the security cameras praying that Violet would make it home safe. I was so tired, my eyelids felt like they wore one hundred pounds a piece. My head bobbed every time I fell into a slight doze, but I quickly awakened because I needed to be awake once she got in. Finally I saw a car coming up the drive way. I put on my slippers and went outside. Violet got out of the car and blew a kiss to the jerk in the driver seat. That little sneaky snake Andrew. I knew she was with him. I really couldn't stand him. Violet was such an airhead when it came to that fool.

She sachet up the rest of the drive way like she owned the place. That ugly boy must've been pickling her down all day because she was surely full of herself. Oh but I was about to change all of that.

"So I guess you're so grown that you can just stay out 'til the wee hours of the morning and not answer your phone right?"
"My phone died," she lied.
"Please don't get it twisted Violet. Yes, I changed my life around. But that don't make me stupid. And that don't mean that I won't fuck you up. You are in my house and you will respect me.. Do you understand that?"
"Yeah I hear you."
"What?"
"I said I hear you."
"Hold up Violet let me put you on to something. I done had niggas put guns in my face and beat me half to death, so I damn sure ain't bowing down to no seventeen year old," I said.
"But you ain't my mother so I really don't gotta listen to you," Violet said rolling her eyes.
"I know I'm not your mother. Our mother is dead. That's beside the point. You came up here with me because you need to get your act together, and that's what you're gonna do. You're not gonna be coming up in my house all hours of the night, thinking that you are grown. You are not grown Violet. You letting this lil nigga gas you up but don't let him get you fucked up."
"Yeah OK," Violet said turning her back on me while reaching for the door handle.

Before she could grab the doorknob, I kicked her in her back, propelling Violet face first into the door.
"Why you had to sneak me?" Violet asked surprised.
"Oh I snuck you? OK then. Square up," I said putting up my guards.

Violet tried to rush me, but I was just too fast for her. I grabbed Violet by her neck and slung her to the ground.
"Get up," I said to her.

Violet got up trying to compose herself. She put her guards up, attempting to go toe to toe with me. She failed miserably. Her hands were wide apart, giving me even more leeway. Violet swung wildly and missed. I came back with an uppercut, knocking her off of her feet.
"Like I said before you don't want to see me baby girl. I tried to warn you. Now get your simple ass up and go in the house. Look at your nigga though. He ain't even try to break it up and he saw you getting your ass handed to you. You gotta learn how to fight before you talk smart to me. I'm the only queen around this bitch. But you willing to disrespect me for this clown," I said.
"You ain't gotta stay with her, you can stay with me," Andrew yelled from the car.
"Boy take your clown ass home," I said.

Andrew backed out of the drive way and sped off. Violet got up and went in the house with her tail between her legs. She was embarrassed. I whipped her ass in front of her little boyfriend and she ain't know how to take it. Oh well, she deserved it. She went in her room and closed the door. I was just glad that she was home. I knew the type of games these guys play these young girls, and I wasn't too keen on the idea of my baby sister being played. I went to my room and pulled out my bible. I needed some clarity.
"You didn't beat her up too bad," Deon said as he rolled over in the bed.
"Naw. Just enough," I replied.
"You are really crazy. Now bring your crazy ass to bed," Deon said.
"Give me a few minutes. I need to do a little bit a reading first," I said to him.

He didn't respond, he just rolled back over. I took my Bible and went into our master bathroom and shut the door behind me. I sat down on the edge of the bath tub and closed my eyes. A familiar verse popped in my head, so I turned to it. Proverbs 29:15 The rod and reproof give wisdom; but a child left to himself bringeth his mother shame.

      This was a powerful one indeed. Sometimes you had to put the big hand to a child to get your point across. Discipline is key, you have to let them know right from wrong. I could've just let it slide, but then what? Then I would've had to deal with Violet thinking that she was the boss, and she would just run all over top of me. No I wasn't her mother, but at this point I was filling those shoes. I knew that if Mama was alive, she would've done the same thing. I closed my Bible said a prayer, then went and got in bed with my husband and kids.

CHAPTER 6: It Will Get Better

I laid in the bed with Deon, trying to get some much needed rest. The kids were in school, and I had dropped Summer and Baby Deon off at my daycare center earlier that morning. As soon as my eyes had closed, my phone rang.
"Oh my goodness all I want is some rest," I said.
"Well just don't answer it," Deon replied.
"No hand it here, it might be important," I said.

Deon handed me my phone from the nightstand. I looked at the screen. It was Violet's school.
"Oh Lord," I said before I answered it. "Hello."
"Hello, may I speak to the parent or guardian of Violet Lee?"
"Yes this is she," I said.
"Hi this is Mrs. Dulaney calling from God's Chosen Ones Christian Academy, how are you this morning?"
"I am fine thank you. And you?"
"I'm good, thank you. Well I'm calling to inform you that Violet has been suspended from school for fighting. She can return to school on Monday, with a parent or guardian present for a conference."
"Fighting? Oh my goodness I'm on my way," I said to Mrs. Dulaney hanging up.
"What's going on?" Deon asked.
"Violet is suspended from school until Monday for fighting. And on top of that I'm gonna have to go up there for a conference once she goes back," I responded.
"Oh boy you got something on your hands."
"Tell me about it."

I drove to the school totally pissed off. Once I got there, I went in and signed her out and told her to come on. On my one day that I had planned to rest my tired body, she had to go and get suspended. We got in the car and she leaned over to the window, like she had an attitude.
"So you get in my car with an attitude because *you* got suspended for fighting? Now how ironic is that?"
"It wasn't my fault," she said.
"So what happened?" I asked.

"She said something about Mama."
"What? So you fought somebody because they said something about your mother, and she doesn't even know her? Are you serious? What? I thought you were in the eleventh grade, not this first grade! Come on now Violet. You can't be for real."

    I couldn't believe the stupidity that I was hearing. She was really fighting because somebody said something about our mother, who was dead and gone? I mean why did that matter? Mama couldn't be hurt about it, she was dead!
"Everybody else got the perfect situation! They got their parents! What I got?"
"A lot! You are not the only one that don't have their parents Violet. Look at me! I ain't go no parents either! I don't even know who my father is! At least you know where you came from! If I even began to tell you the pain that I suffered over the years because of all the bad decisions I have made, not to mention the consequences that I had to face, your head would spin! At least you ain't homeless! At least you ain't gotta worry about eating or having what you need! Your life would be a whole lot easier if you would just enjoy being your age. Stop trying to be grown. It's hard out here. Get focused while you are still young so you won't have to see the real struggle. Stop worrying about that dude because he ain't worried about you. It ain't gon' last Violet trust me, believe what I say. Get your head right and stay in them books so you can have a career and you can be good without a nigga. I'm telling you what's good! Now I know you miss Mama. I miss her too. It ain't a day that goes by that I don't think about her, I think about her all the time. I think about the times I lied to her, and the times I did the complete opposite of what she told me to do. I wonder how things would've been if I had told her that I loved her more. If I wouldn't have been so rebellious against her. I feel so much guilt because I didn't even see her before she died. Yeah I feel all of that, it eats me up inside. But you know what I do? I pray and I ask God to help me be strong. I ask him to hold me when I feel alone and He does it. You may not be old enough to relate to this yet, but I pray that one day you can. I am so petrified

that you are gonna go down the same road that I went down. It would tear me apart to see you going through all that. It may seem like I'm being hard on you or strict and maybe I am but it is for a reason. I want the best for you. The best V. Nothing but the best. But you gotta want the same thing for yourself."
"I'm not no punk I'm not going to let anybody say anything to me and let them get away with it," Violet replied.
"I will be so glad when you grow up because your logic is all screwed up. Let me tell you something about the world and the people in it. You can not control anybody. People are going to do and say whatever they want. If you think you are going to fight somebody every time they say something that you don't like, then you will be fighting all your life. And let me tell you something else. The way this world is now, every body ain't for that fighting stuff no more. Some people would rather shoot and stab. And it's hard to tell whose who until you are already in the situation, and can't get out. I'm telling you Violet you better choose your battles wisely, that life ain't for everybody. You better get your mind right," I said.
"Why do you always have to preach for everything? Just let me live my life! You lived yours didn't you?"
"Violet.. Little girl... You think you know but you have no idea at all. Yes I Lived mine but I wish that I would've listened to Mama and Aunt Lucinda. I could've avoided a lot of the nonsense that came my way if I would've just listened! A hard head makes a soft ass Violet. Seriously. You better tread light, I'm telling you right now. I earned my stripes so I can talk all I want. I have gained my wisdom through a hell of a lot of experiences. And another thing. You better act like you got some damn sense when you are in that damn school, because I am spending my damn money trying to make a better life for your simple ass! Now when we go up there for that conference on Monday you better have a new attitude because I'm telling you I will bust your ass right there in that school. You got it?
"Yeah," she mumbled.
"Um excuse me! I can't hear you!"
"Yes," she said.

Once we got home I let Violet know that she was to do her homework, and then clean the bathroom. She was pissed, her body language was saying it all. But I didn't care. We had to nip that thing in the bud. I wasn't trying to be dealing with this for the rest of he school year. And I damn sure wasn't trying to risk wasting my money on that school if she was going to wind up getting put out for acting like a fool.

I didn't want Violet to go through life acting out every time somebody said something that she didn't agree with. Look at what I did when Franko died. I straight packed up and moved to another state just because I didn't like the things that people were saying about what happened. I let gossip run me away, and that's just not how you handle things in life. You have to hold your head high, and ignore the nonsense because at the end of the day, the only person who really knows whats going on with you is you regardless of what others think they know.

It really bothered me that my little sister took my advice as me trying to preach to her. All I was trying to do was save her some heartache and pain. Being that I have been through a lot, there were just certain things that I knew. How could I say that I loved her and not warn her of the dangers up ahead? What kind of big sister would I be if I just let her run out into traffic? Gosh these young girls out here are just so stubborn and blind at the same time. They wouldn't know danger if I slapped them in the face. It's like when they get a certain age they just let their hormones lead them and nothing else. They will run through a burning building just to get a wet tail. They will jump off a cliff just to prove that they are about something. All I wanted was the best for Violet. I would not be able to sleep at night if I knew she was out in the world like I was, so I had to do everything in my power to make sure that she didn't go that route. And I know some of you are probably saying, "she was only fighting in school it's not a big deal." But you are wrong. See that's where it starts, not being able to exercise some self control. If you can't control your anger when someone says something about your mother, how are you gonna control yourself when a boy tells you he wants you to have his baby? How are you going to control the urges of peer pressure when you can't even control yourself? In life everything you do is like a snowball effect. Everything relates to each other in one way or another. Small mistakes turn into big mistakes if you don't correct them in the beginning.

    I got back into the bed with Deon and let out a sigh. What a wonderful way to spend my off day. Scolding a teenager who clearly knows better. Well maybe she didn't, because like the saying goes, "if you knew better you would do better." Deon wrapped his arms around me and held me tight. I melted into his arms. I really needed his support more than ever. I had a sneaky suspicion that there was going to be a lot more bumps in the road when it came to Violet. But no matter what I wasn't going to give up on my sister. Our mother was gone, so I felt like it was my responsibility to make sure that Violet stayed out of the line of fire. I was going to make sure of that, if it was the last thing that I did.

"You're doing a good job," Deon whispered in my ear.

"Really?" I asked.

"Yes. It'll get better," he responded.

CHAPTER 7: Crazy

    I was so excited to finally be able to spend some quality time with Deon. He called me after he was done at practice and said that he would be home in a hour. I couldn't wait for him to walk through the door. I was ready to jump in his arms and smother him with hugs and kisses. Deon had brought out the affectionate side of me for sure, and I loved him for it. I was starting to get used to the whole idea of having another child in our household too, even though the way the whole situation came about was crazy to say the least.

    But as the day went on, I couldn't help but wonder where Deon was. He told me that he would be home in an hour, and that hour had come and gone. I was starting to get worried, so I called his cell phone. No answer. I didn't know what to think. Was he hurt or was he dipped off in a hotel with some groupie hoe? I couldn't fathom what I would do if I found out that he was cheating while I was home taking care of the kids. I had to do something to get my mind off of all the what ifs. So I cleaned the kitchen, then got the kids ready for bed. They wanted to sleep in Violet's room, and I guess she was feeling nice that evening because she told them yes. Violet had an idea to have movie night with them, so I popped some popcorn and got some snacks together for them to take up to her room. After I had them all situated, I went back downstairs and sat in the living room waiting for Deon to come home. Finally I heard him fumbling around at the door. I jumped on his case as soon as he peeped his head into the dining room.

"So that was a long hour," I remarked.
"I'm sorry but babe you would not believe what happened today," Deon said dropping his bag on the floor.
"What could have happened to cause you to be five hours late for dinner?" I asked.
"Rosie I'm telling you that girl is crazy."
"What girl?"
"Deon's mother," Deon replied.

"OK, but I told you that when she dropped him off here in a wet diaper and without any clean clothes. But I'm still not understanding what her being crazy has to do with you coming home late," I remarked.

"Look. I was ready to leave practice, and when I got to my car she was standing there waiting for me. She got on that same stuff that she was on when she had came to the training camp that time. She was talking about we needed to be a family for our son and all this other crazy shit. So I told her I ain't have no interest in being with her, and that Deon was fine with me and you taking care of him. Then she starts going off talking about she wants her son back, and you better not be making him call you Mommy and all this other crazy talk. So at this point I was tired of talking to her, so I told her to get away from my car."

"OK... So you still ain't get to the point yet," I remarked.

"Just listen. So I kinda moved her to the side so that I could get in my car because she was blocking the door. All of a sudden she started hollering talking 'bout I hit her in her stomach and she was calling the police. So I'm trying to figure out what the fuck she is talking about. Not even three seconds later the girl pulls her phone out and calls the police!"

"What?"

"I couldn't believe it! She was on the phone talkin' bout I hit her and she was pregnant with my baby and she's having a miscarriage-"

I interrupted him, "Hold up. She's pregnant?"

"No just let me tell you the story," Deon said.

"So you still sleeping with her?

"No Rosie. No just listen to the story."

"Go ahead," I said.

"So the police flew over there like they couldn't wait to lock me up once she said my name. So when they get there I'm trying to explain to them that she was lying, and they weren't trying to hear nothing I was saying! She tells them the same lie all over again, then she points to her pants talking about look she's is bleeding, she's having a miscarriage-"

"What?" I interrupted again.

"Just listen Rosie. They called her an ambulance. They locked her up and took me down the bookings. Man long story short she gets down the hospital and once they checked her, they figured out she wasn't having no miscarriage. She was on her period!"

"What? It's really something wrong with that girl," I responded.

"I know! I mean she hates me that much and wants to see me in jail so bad that she came outside while she was on her period, with no pad on.... Just so she could fake a miscarriage and say that I caused it? I'm telling you Rosie I ain't never seen no shit like that in my life."

"So why didn't you call me and let me know what was going on?" I asked him.

"I didn't feel like hearing you zap out and it was going to be too much to explain all this over a jail phone. I knew you were gonna have questions from A to Z and I didn't have all that time to be trying to explain. I just got straight on the phone with Miley so she could get everything under control. You know, be on stand by just in case I needed bail money or whatever. But everything wound up turning around on her."

"You always got some drama with you boy," I replied.

"You act like it was my fault."

"That's not even the point. Every time I turn around one of your ex's is doing something to try to make themselves relevant. It's always drama."

"OK. Rose. Imma just give you some time to yourself because it seems like you have an attitude."

"I don't want time to myself. I want to enjoy my husband. I get sick of having these random little situations popping up with them. You don't think I have the right to have an attitude? I've been sitting at this table waiting for you to come in, not knowing what was wrong or what was going on!"

"Rose I said I was sorry but it really wasn't my fault-"

"I don't care whose fault it was I'm still pissed off about it so stop telling me it wasn't your fault! I am trying to deal with this situation like a grown woman but it's always something! All I wanted to do was have some quality time with you and I couldn't even get that because you were sitting in jail. And all this is happening because you chose to impregnate a psycho," I said before I stormed off upstairs.

    I can't put into words how upset I was. It's hard when you are doing your best to get on the right path and every time you turn around it's stuff coming at you left and right trying to knock you off that path. And it feels even worse when it's somebody else's drama that has you all wound up. He had to do something to get these dummies in check or I was going to wind up catching a case, which I definitely couldn't afford to do. That would jeopardize my child care license, and I couldn't have that. But how much more of the foolishness could I take before I exploded? Only time would tell.

    I got in the bed and pulled the comforter up to my chin. That was my way of saying I didn't want to be bothered without actually saying it. Deon came upstairs and sat on the bed beside me. For a few minutes he didn't say anything, then he started to talk.

"Babe I know this is hard for you. But trust me, this is just as hard for me. But I want you to know that I appreciate you and everything that you do for me and my sons. You are a great wife and mother and I love you. That's why I make sure that you have everything that you want and need. You are my wife and I know that this isn't the easiest situation for you to deal with, so anything that you want I will provide. You know that right?"

    I rolled over so that my back was facing him. He pissed me off when he gave me those speeches, because I knew that he meant what he was saying. I couldn't go against anything that he was saying. He really was a good father and husband. But that was besides the point. I needed some type of relief from all the chaos.

"Rosie do you hear me talking to you? Are you ignoring me? Baby please don't be mad at me. What is it going to take for you to stop being mad at me?"

I began to think. Maybe a new car. Maybe a bigger house, or two new cars would be nice. Nah, that wouldn't solve anything. Like I said before I needed some peace of mind. I needed some relief. So I finally thought of something.
"You need to call your lawyer and figure out what it is that you need to do to keep that girl away from you and this house," I said.
"You mean like a restraining order or something?" he asked.
"Yup. That would probably do you some good."
"Why would I do that? What do I look like getting a restraining order on a female? I'm not scared of her."
"And neither am I. But we both have too much to lose in this situation. Deon she is getting crazier and crazier. I wouldn't put nothing past her, I really wouldn't. This is not going to be the last of you seeing her, trust me. And the last thing you need is her doing something else crazy and getting away with it this time. You can't afford to go to jail or to get sued. And neither can I. You have to do something about this because it is really getting out of hand."

Life lesson eight billion and one; the male ego is a ridiculous thing. This man would rather have this crazy girl stalk him and have him arrested on false charges, than to go and get some papers on her dumb ass just to cut down on the confusion. Men say that women like drama, but in some cases I beg to differ.
"OK Rose. If that's gonna make you happy then that's what I'll do," he said.
"Deon you are missing the point. Are you not seeing the bigger picture here? Am I not painting a vivid enough picture for you? This is not just about making me happy, it's about protecting what you have worked so hard for... Your career and your family. You don't want to be somewhere with kids and this dummy just pop up out of nowhere trying to beef do you? You don't want her to try to run up on me because I will definitely be going to jail! It's all about c.y.a. You gotta cover your ass Deon damn use your brain sometimes," I ranted.

"Girl why can't you just learn to shut up? OK I heard what you said, I'm going to call the lawyer in the morning! You will talk a nigga to death!"

Oh no this nigga didn't! Did he have the balls to raise his voice at me after all I had to put up with? He must've lost his damn mind. But I definitely was about to help him find it. "First of all if you are going to address me then you better do it properly. I am a grown woman, no where near a girl. Them bitches you got them other kids with are girls that's why they always like to keep a bunch of bull shit going on. But let me tell you something. Don't you ever come off at me like that again. I ain't do shit to you but tell you like it is. If you don't like to hear the truth then I advise you to file for a divorce now because I ain't into sugar coating shit. So you better watch your tone before I choke you out in this damn house you know damn well you don't scare me so all the raising of the voice is really uncalled for."

Deon looked at me like he wanted to jack me up seriously. But I didn't back down, I gave him the evil eye right back, without blinking. Then all of a sudden out of no where, he pushed me back on the bed and started kissing me. I wanted to keep up the tough girl role, but it just wasn't working in this situation. It was time for me to give in. There it was, the white flag was up. Suddenly I forgot what we had been arguing about in the first place. With every piece of clothing that came off, I was even more eager to remove the rest. Once we were both in our birthday suits, Deon put his head between my legs without hesitation. I moaned in ecstasy. Deon still hadn't lost his touch, after all the years that I had been getting in the bed with him. Actually, I think he had gotten even better since we were married. Maybe it was all in my head, I don't know. All I know is that after I climaxed, he flipped me over and went to work. I tried to contain myself but I couldn't. The feeling was too good to remain silent. Deon wrapped my hair around his fist and pulled my head back.

"This is what you wanted right? That's why you been acting up right?" he whispered into my ear.

"Yes," I moaned.
"Well next time just ask me and I will give it to you," he continued to whisper grinding deeper inside of me.

It is amazing how much a man can control a woman with sex. Yes we hold the power, but once you have that one that knows how to use his, you will be completely love struck. I honestly believe that I fell in love with him the very first night that I gave myself to him in the V.I.P. room, but my love of money overpowered it. It was just too ironic that the same man that carried me over to the dark side, pulled me into the light also. Now I couldn't see no other man besides him, I couldn't even think of it. I couldn't imagine another man touching me in the places that Deon did.

"Now tell Daddy you are sorry," he went on whispering.
"I'm sorry daddy," I said, giving all my power away.

He had won this round for sure. But I had the rest of our lives to dominate. Good thing we had long hallways, and that the TV. In Violet's room was blasting or those kids would've heard me for sure. Nothing like a good rumble in the sheets to end an argument. I was truly satisfied.

After we finished we laid in bed in silence. These were the moments that I lived for. Laying with my head on his chest, listening to his heart beat while he ran his fingers through my hair. What did I do to deserve this? Sure we weren't perfect, but I mean what is? But the love was there, and there was no denying that. I closed my eyes ready to drift off to sleep and then Deon woke me up with a question that I just couldn't believe.

"Can we have another baby?" he asked.

My eyes popped open so quick that you would've thought I didn't have eyelids. I had to make sure that I heard him correctly.

"What did you say?"
"Can we have another baby?"
"Um... Deon... Summer is still an infant. Are you serious?"

"Yes I'm serious. You're a good mother, and I want to have a few more kids with you," he replied kissing me on the forehead.

"What you tryna make the Brady Bunch over here? I'm still tryna snap back from Summer and you tryna knock me up already? I don't know about that Deon," I said.

"Well just think about it babe. Please?" he asked.

"I guess I can think about it," I remarked.

"OK. I love you."

"I love you to," I said.

    I slept with one eye open that night. I didn't need him trying no sneaky stuff. You know men trap women with babies too right?

CHAPTER 8: Crazier

Well Deon actually listened to me and talked to his lawyer about getting a restraining order on Mocha. He agreed that it was a good idea as well. So after all the necessary paperwork was filed, about a week later it was time for them to go before a judge to decide if the order would be final or not. If so, it would last one year to the day that the judge granted it to be final. Deon looked liked he still didn't want to go through with it. He dragged his feet all morning like he was trying to be late or something. I felt myself getting pissed off, but I had to keep my composure. I surely didn't want an argument to pop off before he had to go to court. So I went on about my morning like I usually did. I dropped off the kids to school, then I took Summer to the daycare center. After that, I headed over to the courthouse to meet Deon there as we had discussed the night before.

  Once I got there, Deon and his lawyer were already in the court room. I sat a few seats behind them, then looked around for Mocha. She was nowhere in sight. I hoped that she showed up because if she didn't more than likely that mean that she hadn't been served and we would have to come back again next week. I wanted this process to be done and over with a.s.a.p. My phone vibrated and I looked at it discretely. It was a text from Rochelle. I didn't want the bailiff to see me with it because phones were supposed to be turned off while in the court room. So I held it down low where he couldn't see it. Then I opened up the text.
Ro
You there yet?
  I decided that I would answer so that Rochelle wouldn't keep sending me the same text over and over again. I love her to death, but when she wants the scoop on something, she wants it right away!
Me
Yeah I'm here.
Ro
What is moose face looking like early in the morning? Lol.

Me
Lol. Girl she ain't here. Hopefully her crazy ass is just running late. But look Imma hit ur phone as soon as we get out of here. You know your phone is supposed to be off when ur in here.
Ro
Ard. Hit me as soon as u leave.
Me
Ok nosy damn! Lol.
Ro
Lol

    I turned my phone off and stuck it in my purse. And if the term "speaking of the devil" didn't fit exactly in this moment, I don't know what did. Mocha switched her swamp monster looking behind into the court room, like she was Ms. America or Beyonce.... Or somebody that she clearly was not. One look at this fool and I was totally embarrassed for her. I mean she just didn't know how to turn the stripper in her off. I mean who really wears a tube top, mini skirt, and thigh high boots to court? Then she had some platinum blond hair in her head, with one side shaved looking like a plucked chicken. This girl had to be on something. And if she blinked her eyes one more time I just knew she was going to fly away with those eyelashes that looked like she had two bat wings glued to her face.

    Oh my goodness I couldn't wait to get out of there so I could call Rochelle and tell her about this. Goodness gracious. Even when I was stripping, I would never have came to court looking like I just left work or like I was on my way there. But you couldn't tell her she wasn't hot though. I laughed to myself anticipating what would happen next. So the clerk began to speak and the foolishness began.

"When I call your name please respond here or present. Please forgive me if I mispronounce anyone's name," the clerk said.

    I looked over at Mocha, and she was looking at herself in her phone screen. If I had a face like hers I would never look at myself, but hey that's neither here nor there.

"Deon Matteo," the clerk went on.

"Present with counsel," Deon's lawyer responded.
"Shamekera Brown," the clerk said.
"Yup yup I'm here I don't need no introduction," Mocha blurted out.

The clerk looked up from the paper work that was in front of her, with a look of confusion on her face. It was taking everything out of me not to bust out laughing. This was going to be good. I glanced over at Deon, who was shaking his head. I could not wait to joke him once we got out of there. Anyway, once the judge came in and took her seat, Deon and Mocha's case was called. My stomach dropped, and I said a silent prayer asking God to let everything go in our favor. So the judge asked to hear Deon's side of the story first. Deon's lawyer started to speak, and then here came the dummy opening her mouth.
"Um excuse me your honor but how is he gonna tell you what happened when he wasn't even there?"
"Ms. Brown that is the job of his counsel, you will have a chance to speak. Please do not interrupt," the judge said looking over her glasses.

And it just got worse and worse. This girl just didn't know when to quit. Every time Deon or his attorney tried to speak, dumb-dumb would interrupt with what seemed to be her favorite line.
"That's a lie your honor, can I talk now?"

Finally the judge seemed as if she was fed up. She took off her glasses and sat them down. Oooh it was about to go down.
"Ms. Brown, this is the last time that I am going to tell you that you need to be quiet, or you will be held in contempt of this court. Do you understand?"
"OK," Mocha responded.

When it was finally her turn to tell her story, for me it was like watching a plane getting ready to crash. I already knew that this was about to be a disaster, but I just had to watch. This girl was coo coo for coco puffs for real. I sat on the edge of my seat, waiting for her to speak, and finally she did.

"I went to see him to talk to him about our son and to ask him when he was going to come back home. I had just seen him three days before that when he stayed at our house," she lied.

Or maybe she wasn't lying. Well let me correct that statement. Maybe in her mind she wasn't lying. Clearly the girl was delirious, I mean the way she was talking she was clearly convinced that what she was saying was true.

"When I got there, he started screaming and yelling at me and then he hit me in my stomach and I started having a miscarriage. So that's when I called the police and they locked him up," she went on. "Your honor I don't have time for all this confusion, I just want my son back. My cousin just died like a two months ago, I really don't have time for all this drama."

I damn near fell out! That girl was a pure nut! Deon looked like he was about to explode any second. I really wished that I had some popcorn because this was too juicy to watch without a snack.

"OK.... So.. do we have a copy of the police report?" the judge asked.

"No I left it at home," Mocha said.

"You honor I have a copy of the police report. Actually there were two. One was written at the beginning of the incident, and one at the end. You will see that Ms. Brown made a falsified statement. She was never hit by Mr. Matteo, and she was not pregnant either. And for the record Mr. Matteo hasn't had any sexual contact with Ms. Brown since they conceived their son, which was three and a half years ago. Mr. Matteo is now married. His wife is here with him today," Deon's lawyer stated as he handed the police report to the bailiff, and then pointed to me.

Yes! That's what I was talking about! He was on point just like he should've been. Nut ball lady was so busy hallucinating that she didn't even think about the fact that when police get involved, everything is documented. The bailiff handed the documents to the judge and she began to read them. I already knew where this was going. After a few minutes, she put the papers down and began to speak.

"Ms. Brown, I want you to hear me clearly. You put up your right hand and swore under oath that your testimony would be nothing but the truth. After reviewing all the evidence I have determined that I am going to grant Mr. Matteo's motion for a final protective order. You are not to contact, or threaten Mr. Matteo, or any of his family. You are to stay away from from his residence and his place of employment. Custody of Deon Matteo Jr. will remain as stated in the custody order issued by the circuit court. This protective order will remain in affect until-"
"That shit ain't fair! The only reason why shit is going his way is because he is famous and he got money! I bet if I was famous then you would be on my side!" Mocha blurted out.
"Do not interrupt the judge again or you are going to be held in contempt!" the bailiff yelled.
"Fuck both of yall,"Mocha said as she took a few steps toward the judge.
  Before she could get any further, the bailiff rushed her, knocking her to the floor. I covered my mouth to keep from laughing out loud. That girl was certified! I never saw anything like that in my life! Mocha was handcuffed and escorted out of the court room. The judge shook her head and looked at Deon.
"Mr. Matteo, I hope that this is a lesson to you. A one night decision can affect you for the rest of your life. I truly feel for you. You made a terrible mistake. You can go pick up a copy of your order from room 108. Have a good day."
"Thank you," Deon said.
"Thank you your honor," his lawyer replied.
  Wow, that was truly a sight to see, literally. I walked over to Deon and gave him a hug. I couldn't help but notice the look of disgust on his face.
"What's wrong?" I asked him.
"I feel bad for my son. I can't believe that I brought a child into the world with somebody like that," he said.
"It's OK babe. You live and you learn. You wouldn't be human if you didn't make any mistakes," I said.
"True."

"Well do you want me to wait with you?" I asked him.
"Naw you can go ahead. I'll just see you at the house. I know you gotta call Rochelle nosy ass and give her all the details," he replied.
"You don't know what I'm going to do stop acting like you know me. See you in a little bit," I said before I walked away from him.

But he did know me indeed, because as soon as I walked out of the courthouse, I turned my phone back on and dialed Rochelle's number. As soon as she answered the phone I spilled my guts about everything. Rochelle laughed and giggled at the whole story, just as I thought she would. Hearing Rochelle's laugh while telling a story always made telling the story much more enjoyable.
"The girl looked like she was about to go hit the block," I said. "I know a few niggas tried to pick her up walking downtown looking like that."
"Are you serious?" Rochelle asked in disbelief.
"If I'm lying I'm flying! Girl then she had the nerve to have on this bright blue eye shadow looking like Mi Mi from off of the Drew Carey show," I said.
"Hahahahahahahahahahahahahahahahahahahahaha girl shut up!"
"Ain't nobody gon' tell me she ain't lost her mind. Ro that girl is really out to lunch. I'm not even mad at her anymore. I feel bad for her, because she has totally lost touch with reality," I said.
"Wow," Rochelle replied.

I chit chatted with Rochelle all the way home. Once I got there I ended the phone call so that I could make a big brunch for Deon, I felt like he deserved it. I thought about calling our personal chef over to whip him up something nice, but Deon always liked it better when I cooked. So I kicked off my pink stilettos and got to work. Half way into it, Deon came in.
"You must've read my mind, 'cause I'm starving," he said before he kissed me on my cheek.

"I kind of figured you were since you didn't eat anything for breakfast," I replied.

"See that's why I got you in my corner. You know what I need even before I do."

"So I know you even better than crazy horse that was at the courthouse?" I teased.

"I knew you was going to bring her up. Man...... She needs some help for real," Deon laughed.

"But for real Deon. Can you do me a favor?" I asked.

"Sure babe wassup?"

"The next time you are trying to get back at me, can you at least upgrade?"

"Stop being smart and hook that food up woman," Deon laughed before he went upstairs.

Yeah he thought I was being smart, but I was dead serious. How did he think he was getting back at me with a piece of trash like that? Men are so simple.

CHAPTER 9: Mrs. Clause

The Christmas season had started to grow on me. When I was a little girl, I never cared for it too much because I never really got much. Mama was always struggling with bills so it was a bit of a stretch for her to be spending money on toys. But now things were so much different than back then. I was in the position to give my family whatever they desired. That was what I loved the most about how I was living. My kids didn't have to go without like I did. Being able to be a provider to my family in an honest way really did bring me joy. I also loved the Christmas season because that meant it was almost time for Summer's birthday. My baby was turning one that year, and I was super excited. So the plan was to fly all of our immediate family out to Hawaii to celebrate her first birthday. I know that's kind of extravagant for a one year old, but hey we had it so why not?

Winter break at the daycare was scheduled to begin two days before Christmas Eve, so I decided to stop in to see how things were going. When I got there, things were looking good as usual. Crispy clean surroundings and happy children, which we all know I loved to see. After speaking with Shanika I felt like I had left no stone unturned, so it was time for me to roll out. I walked past one of the classes and peeped in, where Ms. Johnson was consoling one of the kids.
"Awww what's wrong with him?" I asked her.

She put her finger up motioning me to wait a second while she got him in order. I stood there until she came with me. The kids were all working on Christmas cards for their parents.
"Um.. Well, Gary was crying because he's not going to get anything for Christmas," Ms. Johnson said.
"Well how does he know that?" I asked.
"Here's the thing. When I told the children that we were going to make Christmas cards, he bust out crying. When I asked him what was wrong, he said that his Mommy said Christmas costs too much money so they're not getting anything."
"Who is *they*?"

"His brothers and sisters."

      I instantly felt that sting that I used to feel when me or my sister didn't get anything for the holidays. It wouldn't sit right with knowing that somebody's children were going to be crying on Christmas day because they didn't get a single thing. True I know what the real reason for Christmas is, and it's definitely not about getting anything. It is about the birth of Jesus Christ. But at the same time, they were kids and I could identify with their pain.

"Oh OK. Wow. Well who is his mother so I can talk to her about helping her out for the holidays?"

"I believe her name is Elaina. She has a few other kids and a baby that are enrolled here I believe," Ms. Johnson responded.

      Why, why, why? Why did this child have to belong to Elaina?

This wasn't going to be as easy as I thought. It's a shame when being a good Samaritan gets turned into something difficult.

"OK. I will be here first thing in the morning so I can talk to her. And do me a favor, keep this between us okay?"

"Yes mam," Ms. Johnson said.

      The next morning I got Summer and Baby Deon ready and took them over to the daycare with me. I was going to drop them off so that I could finish up packing for Hawaii, and tie up any other loose ends before we went on the trip. After taking the babies to their designated area I sat in Shanika's office until I saw Elaina arrive with her children. I thought it would be a good idea to wait for her to get her crew settled before I approached her about anything. So, I peaked out of the office so that I would be able to catch Elaina before she dotted the door. Finally I saw my opportunity, and I took it.

"Elaina," I called out to her as quietly as I could.

      Elaina turned around to see who was calling her name. When she saw me walking toward her she rolled her eyes. I could tell that I was the last person that she wanted to see.

"Good morning," I greeted her.

"Hi," Elaina replied.

"I don't want to hold you up, but I just wanted to ask you if it was OK for me to get your children a few things for the holidays."
"What would make you want to do that?"

I wasn't going to tell her that her child had been crying about not getting anything for Christmas, I wouldn't dare! She was the type that would beat her child for that, because they were "telling her business" when in all reality, he was just being a kid.
"No reason really, just thought it would be nice that's all.
"Well no and I would appreciate I if you would just mind your business,"Elaina said.
"It's no reason to get upset. If you have somebody willing to help you then take it. I don't want nothing in return and I ain't trying to hold nothing over your head. This is strictly about the kids it's not about you."
"I don't need you to do nothing for my kids."
"OK and I never said you did. Again, this is not about you it's about them," I responded.
"Whatever. You ain't no friend of mine so I don't want nothing from you. My kids are good, don't worry about it. I hate females that think they better than somebody else-"
"Hold up. Now hate is a real strong word to be trying to use against somebody that's trying to help you. And I ain't never been the type to think I'm better than nobody. I know where I came from and I will never forget it. However, I see that somebody must've pissed in your Wheaties this morning, so it's no point in even trying to reason with the unreasonable. Now you have a blessed day," I said before I walked away from her.

Now usually I would never turn my back on somebody who acted as if they had a problem with me, but at that point I wished she would try it because every kid in there would've witnessed her getting her tail whipped. She really hadn't gotten over what had happened, and for the life of me I still couldn't understand why she was so mad at me? She was the one who put the knife in my back, so I tried to choke the life out of her. I mean what did she expect? But we were kids then, and I couldn't take that back. But she was still salty as the girl on the Morton's salt container. It had to be because Franko died and now she wasn't doing so good, but on my end things were good. But hell, things hadn't always been good! She was truly just on the outside looking in! She thought she knew, but she had no idea. She hadn't seen me when I was tricking or when I was strung out, so she didn't have a clue. But hey if she wanted to be a sour puss that was OK. That didn't mean that I had to be one too. The key to overcoming a nasty disposition is to not let it change you. So I had something right in store for her. I was gonna kill her miserable ass with kindness. It was no way that I wasn't going to be a blessing to someone who was clearly in need, even if they put up a front like they weren't. Besides, God had blessed me greatly, so why wouldn't I pass it on? She must ain't know who she was dealing with. When I have my mind set to do something then I do it. Well she should have known that since she used to be my best friend, but whatever. As soon as she left, I went to the kids classes and looked in their clothes and shoes to see what sizes they wore. I knew that I was going to be taking a shot in the dark about Franko's daughter's sizes since I had never seen her before.

    It was the morning before Christmas, and I had already gotten all of my children's stuff. All of our things were packed for our trip to Hawaii for Summer's birthday celebration/Christmas. Miley had taken care of getting all the gifts over to Hawaii, and I was glad because that was one less task for me to complete. Everybody was excited for the trip. Aunt Lucy would be catching her flight from Baltimore, and Deon's mother would be flying over with Rochelle, the kids and I. Deon's brothers and his nieces and nephews would be flying from Atlanta, and Deon was in New Jersey at the time, so he would be flying from there. There was one last task that I had to complete though: getting the rest of Elaina's children's stuff. I had already gotten their clothes and shoes the day before when Elaina called herself getting smart with me at the daycare. I cringed at the thought of doing last minute shopping, but it had to be done. I decided to take Rochelle with me, because after all two heads are better than one.

"Girl you have really changed, I gotta give you that, if don't nobody else see it, I see it. It ain't no way in hell that I would be buying a bitch that slept with my baby father behind my back kids jack shit," Rochelle said.

"It's not about her Ro, it's about the kids. The kids shouldn't have to miss out just because their mother ain't right. Plus I can't keep holding on to something that happened almost like what... Seven or eight years ago? Girl that would be rotting my own spirit and making my heart hard. You just gotta let some things go," I said.

"True but after she would've tried to get out on me, all that would've went out the window."

"I feel you, but both her and I know what it is... She don't really want no problems, trust me she ain't forget how I bust in that house on her. It's no way she could forget that. I pay all that huffing and puffing no mind, that don't move me none," I said.

We pulled into Toys R' Us parking lot, and it was crowded just as I expected. We were gonna have to roll our sleeves up, get in there, and get to work.

"Now look Ro, I don't want you in here punching people in the face over toys OK? We can not go to jail, we have somewhere to be this evening," I said as we got out of the car.

We both laughed and went into the store. That store had people all over the place. I mean parents were running around like chickens with their heads cut off. Christmas was bringing out the worst in people. There were mother's snatching toys out of other people's carts and some more stuff. I couldn't believe how crazy these people were acting.

"Lord please don't let these people take me out of character," I prayed.

Rochelle and I went down the aisles throwing whatever toys in our carts that we thought the kids might like. About twenty minutes into our spree, pissy Rochelle had an epiphany that she had to use the bathroom.

"Gosh Rochelle why do you always have to use the bathroom when we're out? That's so annoying."

"Well what you want me to do? Be pissy? Girl shut up let me go pee then you can get back to being Mrs. Clause," Rochelle replied.

"Whatever. Hurry up," I responded.

Rochelle went inside the restroom and I stood outside waiting for her. You know that feeling you get when you know someone is staring at you? Well I was getting that feeling. After a couple of minutes, I just couldn't take it anymore.

"Um, do I know you or something?" I asked the short bald guy who was using his eyes like they were microscopes.

"Hey wassup Star," he said grinning like he was cute.

"My name is not Star," I said with confidence.

"You used to work at Show Stoppers, right?"

"Yes."

"Oh OK. I thought so. I don't forget a face. So you *are* star."

This is the moment that I had always hoped would never happen. I never wanted somebody to remember me from the club or the streets. I didn't want anybody to remind me of my dark days. But here I was, having to deal with my past in my present.

"Like I said, my name is not Star. My name is Rose," I said trying to keep my composure.

"Oh, OK I get it. You don't want nobody to know you used to work there. Oh OK. That's cool," he said grinning even harder.

"No. I want to be addressed by *my* name. There is nothing that I can do to change what I *used* to do.

"Well whatever. I know you as Star."

"Correction. You don't *know* me at all."

"It's just like a hoe to act like they more than what they is," he said.

"Boy if you don't go sit your little Humpty Dumpty bald head ass down somewhere. You are totally irrelevant to me. Grow some hair before you talk to me. You ain't fooling nobody you shaved your head because you got a receding hairline. You so worried about who I am you need to be worried about that

kangaroo pouch you got in front of you. Oh! I remember you now! You the one that used to chase me around begging me for a lap dance, but you never had enough money! And you were trying to go in the V.I.P. Room right?"
"Why you so fuckin' loud?" he asked, turning red.
 Who you here with? Your girl? Baby mother? It gotta be somebody because you are clearly standing in front of the women's restroom. I guess you want me to tell whoever she is how you were in love with a stripper?"
"Chill out-"
"Oh OK. That's what I thought. Now beat it baldy before I air you out for real," I said.
 Just then Rochelle came out of the restroom, and a woman holding an infant came out behind her. The look on fatty poo poo's face let me know that was his people. I ice grilled him one more time before I walked off with Rochelle. I didn't even bother to tell Rochelle what had happened. I wasn't even in the mood to repeat the whole story. I was just going to pretend like it didn't even happen. After we finished up there, I remembered that I wanted to get them a Christmas tree.
"Really Rose? A Christmas tree too?" Rochelle asked.
"Um yea... If she didn't have the money for gifts then you know she don't have no tree," I responded.
 After stopping at Wal Mart and purchasing the last tree that they had, and the last of their lights and ornaments our last stop was the grocery store. Christmas wasn't complete without a big dinner of course. I prayed to God that Elaina could cook. Once we pulled up to Elaina's house, it was time to unload all the stuff. She was going to be pissed when she saw all that stuff on her porch. I knew she was gonna figure out that I got her address from her information forms at the daycare. Oh well.
 Rochelle and I started taking all the stuff out of the car and loaded it onto her porch. After everything was on the porch I knocked on the door since there was no bell. I really needed her to hurry up and answer the door because we had a flight to catch at seven, and it was already four thirty. After a about a minute or so, I heard the door unlocking so I started to walk off

of the porch. I didn't even wanna give Elaina a chance to go off, because after that run in with the dude a Toys R' Us my patient was very thin. I heard the door come open as walked down the walkway. I glanced back, and realized that it wasn't Elaina on the porch. It was a little girl. It had to be Franko's daughter because she looked just like him, I mean she was his twin for sure. Eyes, complexion and all. She looked puzzled as all get out. Crap. I couldn't just jump in the car after all.
"Is your Mommy home?" I called out to her.
"No," she said.
      I rushed back to the porch. This little girl didn't have a clue how dangerous it was for her to be saying that out loud. She shouldn't have even been answering the door if her mother wasn't home anyway. And where the hell was Elaina anyway? I really didn't have time for this, I had a flight to catch!
"Sweetie you can not be telling people that your Mommy is not home. You really shouldn't even be answering the door," I said to her.
      She stared at me with a blank expression. I looked past her and into the house, because she had left the door wide open. I was appalled by what I could see through the door way. The house was a despicable mess. Now I had a dilemma. What was I to do now? Just leave with all that stuff on the porch, or take it inside? I couldn't leave it on the porch, not in that neighborhood. Somebody would have a field day with all those toys and clothes, not even to mention the food.
"Ro, come help me take this stuff in the house!" I yelled.
"What?"
"Come on girl!"
      Rochelle got out of the car and walked up to the house. She gave me the craziest look ever. I wanted to bust out laughing, but I held it in. We started to take the stuff in and I couldn't help but to look at my surroundings. Pure filth is how I would describe it. For the life of me I could not understand how a woman could keep a house like that. It was awful. Filthy walls. Carpet full of stains. Trash on the floor. And the smell... Oh Lord the smell.

"So what's your name?" the little girl asked me.
"Mrs. Clause," I said. "What's your name?"
"Hope," she answered.

Now that didn't make any sense whatsoever. Elaina really wanted to be like me. I named my daughter Miracle, and she named hers Hope. What a coincidence.
"But I thought Mrs. Clause was fat and white," Hope said to me.

Wow. This little girl was something else. I saw Rochelle's eyes tearing up from holding in her laugh. She was going to have so many jokes once we got in the car, I could tell. Before I could answer, I heard another child calling her from upstairs.
"Hope! Hope! Tonio bit me!"

Hope immediately ran upstairs to tend to them. I looked at Rochelle in amazement. I couldn't believe what I was seeing.
"You meaning to tell me she got that little girl watching all the kids?"
"That's what it looks like to me," Rochelle said. "Come on girl lets get out of this rat trap."
"Girl I can't leave these kids here by their self! What if something happens?"
"Damn Rose you done turned into Captain Save a Hoe! If she don't care then why should you?"
"Because it's not right that's why! I don't care what she does! It's not about her I keep telling you that! God forbid something happens after I leave here! I couldn't have that on my conscience!"

Just then I heard the front door slam. It looked like I wouldn't have to leave the kids there alone after all. Elaina was home. I turned around to face her, as I could tell that this was not going to be good.
"Why the hell is you in my house?" she asked.
"Look, I came here to bring the stuff that I picked up the kids for Christmas. I sat it on the porch and knocked, and Hope came to the door. I saw that you weren't here and I didn't wanna leave that stuff on the porch so I -"

In the middle of my sentence the kids came running down the steps like a stampede.
"Ma! Do you see all the stuff Mrs. Clause brought us? Even food!" Hope exclaimed.
The look on Elaina's face spoke volumes. She was too through with me. I had brought her children stuff and they were excited about it. How dare I do such a thing?
"Where is the baby?" Elaina snapped at Hope.
"Upstairs in his car seat."
"Well why would you leave him by his self? All yall go back upstairs!" Elaina screamed.
The children ran back up the stairs. Rochelle looked at me and shook her head. Elaina looked at her and frowned up her face.
"And who is this bitch you got in my house?"
"Bitch? See Rose might've changed but I'm still in slap a bitch mode so if you-"
"Ard yall stop! Elaina you are an adult so act like one and not a chicken head okay? This is my best friend Rochelle," I said interrupting the quarrel. "She helped me bring the stuff over here. Anyway, everything is here so we're leaving."
"You got a lot of nerve bringing your uppity ass over here with all this bull shit tryna play Santa Clause. I told you I don't want your shit so take it back with you," Elaina responded.
"Now let me tell you something, Ms. I slept with your man and had a baby so now I'm mad at you. I'm not taking shit back. What you're gonna do is put that damn tree up and put then gifts under it, and you are going to make them kids a decent Christmas dinner. You so busy being bitter, you need to get busy cleaning up this nasty ass house. You ought to be ashamed of yourself, I mean really? You got your six year old baby sitting a house full of kids, including an infant! Come on now Elaina get your shit together! For real! And you need to teach Hope not to open the damn door because I could've been anybody!"
"First of all she is eight, and don't be telling me-"

"I don't give a rat's ass what you talking about Elaina. Clean this house up and get your shit together. And if I find out that you didn't give them kids these gifts, or that you laid a finger on anyone of them I will be calling Child Protective Services to come snatch all of them! Then I will have your ass locked up for child endangerment and neglect for leaving them in here by their self, with your trifling ass! Now if you think I'm playing try me!"

Elaina looked as if she wanted to respond, but she knew what was good for her. She better had kept her mouth shut because she knew damn well she was dead wrong for having those children living like that. It was a pure disgrace. I walked toward the front door, and Rochelle just stood where she was staring at Elaina.

"Come on girl she ain't crazy," I said to Rochelle.
"Oh I was just making sure," she replied.
"Enjoy yall Christmas!" I yelled up the stairs before we hit the door.
"Okay Mrs. Clause!" I heard the kids yelling from upstairs.
"Excuse my french but you a bad bitch!" Rochelle exploded into laughter once we were in the car.
"And you are just crazy," I said with a smirk. "Ard back to the real world. We gotta make this flight, because if we miss it and I gotta buy more tickets, Imma come back over here and rip every one of them raggedy tracks right out of her head."

Rochelle and I laughed hysterically as I pulled off. It's nothing like a little drama to spice things up a bit.

CHAPTER 10: Love, Celebration, and Scandal

The gorgeous blue water and sunny skies. The beautiful palm trees and white sand. Maui, Hawaii was absolutely stunning. I fell in love the moment we touched down. This was going to be great. Fun and family is always a good thing. As soon as we got to our hotel, we fed the kids and got them ready for bed. I needed to get the gifts set up under the tree. I didn't want any help from Deon, there was a special way that I wanted everything set up and only I could do it (well at least that's how I felt). After I was done, I sat down in front of the tree and went deep into thought. How amazing was my life at that very moment? I had the resources to help another family in need and my family was vacationing in Maui. Blessed was an understatement. Deon came and sat down beside me.
"I love you," he said.
"Oh Lord, what did you do?" I asked.
"Nothing. What I can't tell you that I love you?"
"Yea you can, but when you just come out of no where with it I get nervous."
"Anyway, since we make the holidays all about the kids, and since you are the best wife that a man could ever have, I got you something," Deon said.
"Oh really? The best wife a man could ever have?" I asked.
"That's what I said," Deon replied while digging in his pocket.
He pulled out a sheet of folded paper and I was confused until he unfolded it. I looked at it and I felt my smile growing wider and wider. It was a blueprint.
"This is for our home in LA that you wanted," he said.
"Oh my goodness Deon!" I screamed as I tackled him onto the floor.
"So I'm guessing that you like your gift?"
"Yes baby of course I do. Thank you for being a husband that thrives on making all of his wife's dreams come true. I love you," I said before planting a juicy one on his lips.
"Thank you for being my queen," he said after the kiss was over. "But I have something else for you."

Once again, Deon dug in his pocket. This time he pulled out a car key and handed it to me. I had to do a double take after I recognized the emblem.

"A PORCHE?"

"Yup and it's red too. You gon' look so sexy driving it," Deon said.

I couldn't contain myself any longer. I ripped his clothes off of him and transformed into a lioness. My intensity was too much for him, so he gripped his fingers firmly on my hips attempting to slow me down. This sex was phenomenal, just as it should've been. We emptied ourselves into each other underneath the glow from the tree until we were satisfied.

The next day started off perfectly. It was Christmas morning and my baby girl Summer's big day. Man, time had really gotten away from me with this one. My baby was a year old. I was so overwhelmed with joy. All the kids tore open their gifts one by one. I loved seeing their different reactions. This moment was priceless. After they opened their gifts everybody got cleaned up and dressed and we all met up for Summer's birthday breakfast. It felt so good to have everybody together and enjoy each others company. I was really happy to see Aunt Lucinda too.

After breakfast the whole family got suited up and we went to the beach. Everybody knows that kids love the water and will stay in it all day if you let them. I laid out with my bikini on so that I could get a little sun kissed glow. Then I pulled out my pen and pad so that I could do a little writing.

Explanation

To explain this joy I feel inside would be that of something great.
Like a phoenix rising from the flames,
Like wine transformed from a grape.
To explain this peace that I feel would be of something great.
Like a the moon when it is full,
Like a sinner given a clean slate.
To explain this love in my heart would be of something great
Like a newborn placed in her mothers arms,

Like a crooked path finally going straight.
If I was ever given the opportunity to explain my love for you it would be how I even love the things that I dislike about you.
I would say how my sun rises and sets on you,
I would say that I would do anything for you.
I would say that those butterflies never went away,
I would say that I would crumble if you ever went astray.
If I was ever given the opportunity to explain my love for you.
I would say that I could explain it in one word. TRUE.

  The event for the evening to celebrate Summer's birthday was the Old Lahaina Luau. I was so excited to go, I had heard so much about it. And let me tell you, the performances were true perfection. Everyone enjoyed themselves. The fire fire throwers really captivated you with their talent. You had to be a brave man to be playing around with fire like that! The hula girls were beautiful. All the men in our family seemed to be mesmerized by the way the girls moved their hips. That is truly an art I tell you. They wore these huge head pieces, with grass skirts and coconut bras, with their hips moving a mile a minute. Summer clapped her hands like she wanted to get up and dance with them! I knew that the kids would never forget this trip. And the food was out of this world. Forget a buffet, nothing can compare to an authentic luau feast. Hawaiian laulau, mochiko chicken, shoyu chicken, huli chicken, coconut fried shrimp, teriyaki beef, lomi lomi salmon, baked mahi mahi, fresh fruit, and banana pineapple upside down cake were just some of the food on the menu. I had finally stopped nursing Summer, so I had a Mai Tai or two.

  We finally called it a night and everyone went to their own rooms. After our children were in bed, all I wanted to do was sleep. Deon was exhausted too. He fell asleep on me, after all he made all these fabulous plans of what he and I were gonna do after the kids went to sleep. I wasn't mad at him though, I understood that he was tired. I tossed and turned trying to get comfortable, but it wasn't really working for me. I decided to go over to Rochelle's room for some girl talk since I couldn't sleep. She was a night owl anyway, so I knew that she wouldn't mind. I got up and slipped some shorts and a tank top on, then I crept to my door. I opened it and as I stepped out I saw Antoine, Deon's brother, peep his head out of Rochelle's door. When he saw me he hurried up and slammed the door back, too bad I already saw him. I couldn't believe the nerve of them two. First of all, Antoine was married with six kids, and his family was in Hawaii with us. He had the audacity to be creeping with my best friend on what was supposed to be a birthday celebration for my baby? I stood behind my door and looked out of the peep hole. After about five minutes, I saw Antoine walking past. He must've been taking his trifling behind back to his room. I opened the door and walked back over to Rochelle's room. She better not ignore me knocking because I knew damn well that she wasn't sleep.

"Hey what you doing up?" Rochelle asked when she finally answered the door.

"You know I have trouble sleeping in hotels," I said.

Rochelle didn't say anything back. She knew what was up. I already knew that Antoine told her that I saw him, so I guess she was trying to think of something to say to cut the awkwardness. There was nothing she could say that could do that.

"I know you know that I saw Antoine coming out of here," I said.

"Yea," she replied.

"Well I can't tell you what to do because you are grown. And I can't judge you because I've done worse. But come on now Ro. You can do better than that. What can you possibly get out of creeping with a married man?"

"Things just happen sometimes," Rochelle said.

"Yeah they do. But not sex... There are steps that lead up to it that give you ample enough time to stop," I responded.

"It sounds like your judging to me."

"And it looks like you're being stupid to me! Rochelle you been there and done that. Why would you put yourself in that kind of situation? And did you even think about me? This is my family now. If his wife was to ever find out about yall two you know she gon look at me crazy. And you know I ain't gon' let her come up against you, so that's gon' make things even worse! Like, what are you thinking about?"

"I really don't want to talk about this right now," Rochelle said.

"I don't care what you want because obviously you don't care about what I want. I don't want to be keeping secrets from my husband, but I'm gonna have to keep this one because I'm not going to put you out there like that. You just put me in an awkward position for real," I said.

"I didn't mean to do that. My bad," she replied.

"Damn Rochelle, you are real nonchalant right now. Do you realize that if this would've came out then it would've turned this whole trip upside down? This is supposed to be a celebration for Summer, and something for the other kids too. Shit could've really went left and yall didn't care because all yall could think about was a quick screw! Not to mention that's just not right! Yall are doing that up under his wife's nose. God does not like what yall are doing."

"Well excuse me Ms. Righteous, but I do still sin from time to time."

"I knew I wouldn't be long before you tried to throw that up in my face. But I'm not about to apologize for trying to live right. And I'm not going to sit up here and act like what you are doing is OK. True friends are honest with each other, and they ain't gon' sugar coat stuff just to make the other one feel better. You know what can happen when you play home wrecker."

"Oh so now I'm a home wrecker?"

"Yes! Yes you are! You are sleeping with a married man while his wife is in their room with their six kids! You do the math Rochelle!"

"Get out!" Rochelle yelled.

"That's cool. People don't like hearing the truth," I said before I left.

      I stomped back in my room and slammed the door, forgetting that everyone was sleep. Deon rolled over and looked at me like I was crazy.

"What the hell is wrong with you?" he asked.
"Nothing," I lied.

I got in the bed and attempted to go to sleep. It didn't really work though. I couldn't stop thinking about Rochelle and Antoine. They were so selfish for what they did. Since I was married now, I could only imagine how I would feel if I found out that Deon was cheating. Rochelle new better, she really did. You can never get all of a man when he is married, so why would you except just being a jump off? I was really upset because I didn't want anybody looking at my best friend like she ain't worth being somebody's wife. Rochelle was a good person who was way smarter than being crept off in the middle of the night.

I never did go to sleep that night, I was just too wound up. Everyone met up for breakfast again, well everybody except Rochelle.

"Where's Rochelle?" Aunt Lucy asked me.

"I don't know, I guess she's in her room. Maybe she's coming a little late," I said.

I glanced over at Antoine and he was looking just as dumb as a doorknob. His face had guilt all over it. Lucky for him, his wife was too engrossed in all them damn kids that she didn't even pay it any attention. That's just crazy, because if that was Deon I would've picked right up on it. Or at least I think I would've. A woman's name is mentioned and then my husband starts going crossed eyed. Yeah his behavior stuck out like a sore thumb. Or maybe it did to me because I knew what was going on.

After breakfast Deon announced that the men would be taking the children out so that the women could have some time to themselves. That was cool with me, because I needed to try to get some sleep. I ordered a mimosa to go and headed back to my room. After I started to feel my little buzz, I figured that I could get some sleep so that's what I did. After I got up from my nap, I got myself together then went over to Rochelle's room. I wanted to apologize for what I said to her the night before. I may have been a little abrasive in my

approach, and I didn't like to hurt people's feelings especially ones that I love. Her door was cracked so I walked straight in. to my surprise, a housekeeper was inside cleaning up.
"You scared me," she said.
"I'm sorry I was just looking for my friend," I replied.
"Checkout," she said.

I knew what I heard her say, but her English wasn't the best so I wasn't going to ask her to elaborate. I pulled out the top drawer of the dresser and it was empty. I pulled out the second one, and it was the same. In fact, all of them were empty. The closet was empty too. I went back to my room and sat on my bed.
"I know she didn't just leave," I said to myself.

I called her phone, but it went straight to voice mail. I sat on the bed thinking of what to do next and I was hit with the reality that there was nothing that I could do. Rochelle had left this beautiful vacation because I didn't know how to package my feelings. Just then there was a knock on the door. I got up and answered it.
"Hey Rosie, why are you all cooped up in this room let's go have some fun," Aunt Lucinda said.
"I'm not really in the mood for fun Aunt Lucy," I replied.
"What's wrong?"
"Rochelle's gone."
"Gone where?"
"Gone like gone home gone."
"Why? She had an emergency?"
"No..... I said some things that maybe I shouldn't have said. Well let me rephrase that. I didn't express my feelings in an appropriate manner," I explained.
"Oh... I see. So basically you hurt her feelings," Aunt Lucinda responded.
"Yes, I guess you could say that."
"Well a true friendship will have times where the people in it don't see eye to eye. You won't agree on everything. But you have to be considerate of each others feelings. You have to think before you speak, that's when you're talking to anybody.

If you are angry, you should wait until you cool off a bit before you start running your mouth. Once those words come out of your mouth, you can't take them back no matter how hard you try," she advised.

"Yea, I see that now.... well I'm not even gonna say now because I've been known that it's not what you say it's how you say it," I replied.

    Damn I don't like apologizing.

CHAPTER 11: The Showdown

The new year was here and everything was back to normal. Well everything except my friendship with Rochelle, we still weren't speaking. The kids were back in school, and my daycare was back open as well. We hadn't heard from Mocha, and nobody was mad about that at all.... We were still waiting for a court date for the final custody hearing, but other than that everything was cool. Trina had even calmed down a bit, she must've had a knew man or something. If that was the case, then Deon and I hoped that he would marry her to keep her out of our hair.

My day had been going good. The kids were at the table with the their snacks doing their homework, and Violet was helping them. Summer and Baby Deon were playing on the kitchen floor with some pots and pans and I was getting dinner ready.
"V, go get the mail for me please," I called out to her.
"OK," she responded.

Not even two minutes later, Violet came back in the house yelling.
"Rosie some lady is outside talking 'bout yall better give her son back or it's gonna be trouble!"
"What?" I asked.

I was in the middle of slicing some squash, we were having it for dinner. Baked chicken, brown rice and squash to be exact. The fact that she came back pissed me off, but the troll bitch had the nerve to be on my property making threats. Oh hell no it was on now. I ain't care nothing about all those restraining orders. I wasn't thinking about calling no police because if trouble was what she wanted, trouble is what she was gonna get. I took my apron off and put my hair in a ponytail.
"When I leave out of this house don't answer this door for nobody you understand? Go upstairs in Deon's nightstand and grab those court papers. Bring them downstairs. Keep the kids away from the windows. I don't want them to see me beat this bitch ass," I instructed.

"But I wanna fight too!" Violet said.
"No you don't. This ain't cute. But at this point I feel like it's necessary."

I walked to the front door and opened it. There she was, standing there like she was the queen of the world. I walked outside and slammed my door.
"Is it something here that you need?"
"Bitch where is my son?"
"You mean the same son that you sent over here pissy and starving?"
"You ain't got no room to judge nobody," Mocha said.
"Remember I know you."
"No you know who I used to be," I said walking down the front steps.
"Just give me my son, that's all I want."
"What do I look like giving him back to you when you just dropped him off here like he was a piece of trash? If you cared that much about him then you would've never left him on this door step."

The next thing I know, I see the Channel 13 news van pulling up in my drive way. I was trying to figure out what was going on, but I couldn't. Mocha just stood there and laughed. The van parked as I stood there in a daze. A reporter got out of the van, and a camera man ran behind her. She approached me eagerly. I had a feeling that things were bound to get ugly.
"Is it true that you and your husband, quarter back for the Baltimore Ravens Deon Matteo, are holding Ms. Brown's son without her consent?" she began pushing the mic in my face.
"No it's not," I said.
"What do you have to say about the allegations of you being a heroine addict, and not being capable of caring for her child?"

And that's when the nerve was struck. Mocha leaned up against her car smiling. She knew exactly what she was doing. Oh but it definitely wasn't going down like that, not on my watch. She wanted to play dirty, well she was about to feel the repercussions of that.
"Excuse me," I said to the reporter.

"What do you have to say about the allegations-" the reporter began to repeat herself.

"No I meant excuse me like get out of my way excuse me," I said pushing past her.

All I saw was red. I can't even remember exactly what I did. All I know is I punched her in her nose, blood sprayed everywhere, and the next thing I know I was on top of her banging her head against the pavement.

"Get her off of me! Somebody call the police!"Mocha screamed.

"Oh now you want the police bitch? It's gonna take more than the police to help you!" I screamed as I punched her in her face.

Now correct me if I'm wrong but why would this fruit loop be yelling for the police when she wasn't even supposed to be anywhere near my property? That damn Mocha was a special case. After one of the camera men pulled me off of her, I got a kick in before I walked away from her. Mocha slowly stood to her feet with blood pouring from her nose.

"That's OK! Bitch you put your hands on me, now you're going to jail!" Mocha screamed as she pulled her phone out of her pocket and called the police.

I knocked on my door out of breath. I needed to get a copy of the order to show the police when they got there. Violet opened the door, and I went in. She already had the copies in her hand.

"Oh my goodness Rosie it ain't no way she can tell nobody she won that fight," Violet laughed.

"It's not funny V. I let my temper get the best of me. Now this mess is gonna be all over TV," I said trying to catch my breath. "Hand me the phone so I can call Deon."

Violet brought me the phone and I dialed Deon's number. He picked up after one ring.

"Hey baby I'm almost home. Wassup?"

"I just beat up Mocha. You better hurry up and get here, she got the news here and she called the police," I informed him.

"What? I'll be there in five minutes."

I looked out the window and saw the police coming up the driveway. I went back outside in a hurry and left the papers in the house by a mistake.
"Are you Rose Matteo?" One officer asked.
"Yes I am," I said.
"Place your hands behind your back please," he said.
"For what?"
"You assaulted Ms. Brown and we have witnesses here. And you have her child without her permission. Technically, that is kidnap."
"What's wrong with yall? Yall just jump to conclusions! So what her nose is bleeding! She don't belong nowhere around here! My husband has a restraining order on her!"
"She lying!" Mocha yelled with her fake cry.

The other officer pushed me against the car and put the cuffs on me. I thought about fighting him, but he had a gun and I knew how trigger happy these police are these days. After he put the cuffs on me, he sat me on the ground. By this time, the police had asked to reporters to step away from the house, and I was glad. They had close up footage of me beating her up, but none of them locking me up. I put my head down and started to pray to myself. I couldn't let my kids see me in these cuffs. As soon as I lifted my head, Deon was pulling in the driveway. His mug was broke all the way down, I could tell that he was furious. He got out of the car and slammed the door.
"First of all yall need to take the cuffs off of my wife. I have a restraining order against that girl, she's not even supposed to be on my property. I have temporary custody of my son, so no kidnapping was involved. Yall need to see what's really going before yall just start throwing cuffs on people," Deon said handing one of the officers a copy of the order.

The officer began to read it and his face turned red. He realized that he was wrong. Deon stared at him as he continued to read.
"So like I said get them cuffs off of my wife and put them on that crazy bitch over there. Yall didn't even check to see what was going on. She has a history of filing false reports. And

what's yall badge numbers? I got some reporting of my own that I need to do."
"We apologize for this it was a complete misunderstanding-"
"No it wasn't a misunderstanding it was you not doing your job correctly. Baltimore County Police Department is going to be paying me when this is all said and done. So don't be surprised when yall hear from my attorney," Deon said.

The other officer grabbed Mocha and hand cuffed her while I was being uncuffed. Mocha screamed and hollered as she was put into the back of the squad car. After we got our copy of the report, Deon and I went in the house.
"I can't believe that girl, she is really crazy," Deon said.
"Tell me about it," I replied.
"And you just had to go Mayweather on her. Girl you never cease to amaze me," Deon laughed.
"Yeah whatever. Look you're on Daddy duty tonight. Imma go take a shower, finish up this dinner, and then I'm going to bed."
"OK, that's cool. Imma call Rosenburg in the morning."
"Yea please do, because these police definitely got it coming to them," I said before I walked upstairs.

Now after I cooled down, I felt kind of bad about how I beat that girl up. I was a grown woman, and truth be told, I hit her first. Plus, it didn't take a rocket scientist to figure out that mentally she wasn't all there. I really let my emotions get the best of me, and an adult is supposed to have more control than that. Now it was footage of me beating the hell out of Mocha all over TV and that wasn't good at all. Aunt Lucinda called and let me have it once the footage aired. After I explained the whole situation she took it down a notch, but she was still mad.

Then it was my business that I was concerned about. Any of the parents of the kids at my daycare center could have decided pull their child out. They could have easily said that they didn't want their babies going to a daycare that was owned by some ghetto lady that liked to whip ass on the news. But by the grace of God, my business didn't suffer because of the incident. Everything went on as usual, and I was so grateful for that. I had worked too hard to start my business to have it all go down the drain.

You see, if this had been a few years prior, I would've pointed every finger on both of my hands at Mocha. But that's where change and maturity comes into play. With every decision that you make, comes a consequence to follow. Instead of me taking the high road, I decided to stoop to her level when clearly I knew better. You know the saying, "if you knew better, you'd do better"? Well that applied to me in this situation, because I really did know better so I should've done better. This wasn't high school. I was an adult. Anything could've went wrong. One of my kids could've come outside and witnessed the whole thing. My business could've suffered. As crazy as Mocha was, she could've had a weapon and I could've been walking into a trap for all I knew. How would my children have felt if she would've shot or killed me, all over a petty fight? How would my husband feel to know that he was caught in the middle of all that mess? Thank God that none of that happened, but I recognized that it could've. All I had to do was call the police, show them the paperwork, and let them do the rest. But no, I had to be big bad Rosie that couldn't stand the thought of somebody being disrespectful to me. How could I expect her to respect me, when she didn't even respect herself? Anybody who would drop their child off on somebody's doorstep out of spite did not respect them self. Anybody who would lie and try to stir up drama because of envy had some serious soul searching to do, and I could not risk losing everything that I had over somebody like that. She had controlled me just like a puppet in that situation. Mocha knew that I was going to be fed up by her actions and that I was going to lash out. She had it all mapped out. At that moment I decided that would never jeopardize so much ever again.

"You ain't have to beat that girl up like that on national TV," Rochelle said to me after I answered the phone.

I was really surprised to hear from her to be honest. Rochelle and I had gone much longer without speaking before,

but guess that was more on my part than hers. And I really should've called her as soon as I got back to Baltimore, but my pride wouldn't let me. I was happy to hear from her though because I was ready to bury the hatchet. Life was too short to let a few words break up a meaningful friendship.
"Yea I know. I am so embarrassed," I said.
"Why? It ain't like she beat you up."
"I know. I just don't want to be looking like no hood rat on TV. But anyway I'm glad you called. I want to apologize for how I came off at you in Maui."
"I accept. But you aren't the only one that should be apologizing. I should too. So I apologize for putting you in an awkward position. After I really thought about it, I really could've caused trouble between everybody. The last thing I would want to do is to make things messy within your family. So I hope we can move on from this without any hard feelings," Rochelle said to me.
"Of course we can. But there's just one more thing I want to say. I wasn't judging you. And I wasn't looking down on you. It's just that I know you're worth way more than what that situation could ever get you. You are way better than that. So like I said if I hurt your feelings I really do apologize," I said.
"I know. And like I said, apology accepted.

CHAPTER 12: Winners

It was a chilly winter Sunday, Super Bowl Sunday to be exact and I was at the Ravens versus the Patriots game with Violet and the kids. The Ravens were up twenty one to seven, and Deon was looking great. I sipped my glass of champagne thinking to myself about how blessed I was to be living the life that I was. I looked at a few of the other player's wives all huddled up cackling away. I just couldn't get into that. I wanted no parts of the whole football wives clique. A lot of them were bougie as hell, even though ninety percent of them came from the gutter just like me. I just couldn't understand how some folk could forget where they came from, and could have the nerve to turn their noses up at others. It was crazy because they would even speak to me and the last time I checked they didn't even know me to dislike me. But that's just how the cookie crumbles sometimes. You can't always be a part of the in crowd, and in this case I was glad I wasn't because if one of them bougie hoes tried to play with me they would surely feel my wrath. So I just kept doing me, coming to the games with my family to support my husband. That's it and that's all.

So anyway, I was chillin' in my own world, waiting for Violet to come back from the restroom with the kids. That's when I saw one of them Bougie Betty's walking toward me in my peripheral view. I couldn't for the life of me think of a reason why she would be approaching me, but I was ready for whatever though. I turned around to face her before she even had a chance to try to get my attention.

"Hi, I'm Tori Alexander. I am Levelle Alexander's wife. How are you?" she asked with her phoney smile.

"Hi. I know who you are. I'm fine, how are you? I asked her, even though I really didn't give a damn.

"Very well," she said. "Well look I don't want to interrupt you but I have a business opportunity that I think you could take part in."

"I'm listening."

" Basically I just signed a deal with Neiman Marcus. I'm launching a new perfume line called Youth. The tall young lady with you, I see her at all the games with you. She is gorgeous," Tori complimented.

"Thank you," I said.

"Well any way, I'm looking for a model for the line. A fresh face. Would your daughter be interested?"

"That's my baby sister. And I don't know. She never said anything to me about wanting to get into modeling. But she really does have the look. I can talk to her about it. But of course I would need some information from you... Some specifics on what you're planning to do," I answered.

"Oh of course, of course," Tori said. "Well I'll just give you my card. If you guys think that this is something you want to get on board with just give me a call. We can schedule a meeting so we can talk more about it."

"OK that sounds cool," I said.

  I took her card and placed it in my purse. I took another sip from my glass and let my mind drift. This could be a great opportunity for Violet if it played out right. But did I really want to be mixed up with that pointy nosed heifer? I wasn't too sure. So for the rest of the game I went back and forth in my mind about whether I should even mention it to Violet or not. I mean, this lady had never even said hi to me before today, and now she was so eager to do business with me? I just couldn't be too sure. But then I had to weigh my options. Turn down a business opportunity just because I didn't particularly care for the person who presented it to me, or get that money because regardless of how many shades of fake Tori was, money was always green. Hmmmm... I decided to go with option two.

  After the game was over and Deon got cleaned up, we headed out to dinner to celebrate their win against the Patriots. These were the times that I loved. I loved my family. Even though it wasn't always peaches and cream, when things were good, they were great. Deon and I held hands as he drove. The kids laughed and joked as Violet tapped away on her phone. Everyone was in their happy place.

  Dinner itself was just as pleasant as the ride over. Our table was overflowing with seafood and steak. Miracle went on and about how much she loved steak and how she wanted a steak dinner for her birthday. I laughed, because her birthday had just past a few months prior so she had almost a year before her next one rolled around. As we ate and enjoyed each others company, I decided to tell my family about the conversation that I had with Tori at the game. I got everyone's attention.

"Hold up yall I gotta tell yall something," I said grinning.

"What? You're pregnant?" Violet asked.

"No girl bye," I joked. "But seriously I have something to tell yall."

"We're listening," Deon spoke for everyone.

"Well, today at the game LeVelle's wife came over to me and she basically told me that she's starting a new perfume line. And guess who she wants to be the model for it?"

"You?" Miracle guessed.

"Awww wasn't that nice of you to say? But no she wants V," I replied.

"For real?" Violet asked genuinely surprised.

"Yes for real."

"Dag V you gon' be a model and stuff I guess you gon' think you're cute and famous," Lil Franko said chewing his steak.

Everyone laughed. Violet just sat in silence, blushing.

"So what do you think V? You think you would want to do it?" I asked her.

"I... I don't know. I don't know nothing about being a model," she said.

"If you want to do it I can get you a modeling coach that's not an issue," I assured her.

"How much money is Tori talking?" Deon butted in.

"We didn't get that deep into it. I told her I would talk to Violet first, then I could talk to Tori more in depth about it," I informed him.

"Oh OK because we ain't accepting no slouch money. If they want a quality model they better be cutting a quality check, Deon said.

"Deon I got this, you just focus on football okay?"

"Well excuse me Mrs. Momager," Deon joked.

Everyone laughed again. Deon always had a sarcastic comeback no matter what the topic was. I focused back on the subject at hand.

"So what do you think V? Do you think you want to give it a try? I think you will be able to do it if you really want to. I don't want to pressure you though. So if you don't think this is right for you, I can just tell her no," I explained.

"Okay, I'll do it," Violet said.

"You sure?" I asked.

"Yeah. It sounds like it could be fun. Plus none of my friends in VA can say they model for a perfume line," she giggled.

"Well that didn't take a whole lot of convincing," I said.

"Nope, she got that fire in her eye already, she 'bout to be the next Tyra Banks yall!" Deon said.

The whole table burst into laughter. Then a thought popped into my head; I had to call Aunt Lucinda and let her know what was going on. It wouldn't be right not to.

"Ard yall. Let me call Aunt Lucy. Imma put her on speaker," I said before I did just that.

"Hello," she said.

"Hey Aunt Lucy. What you doing?" I asked her.

"Well hey there. I'm no doing much, just baking a few pound cakes for the church bake sale."

"Oh for real? When is the bake sale?"

"Tomorrow. But what you so happy about? I can hear it all in your voice."

"Oh well first I gotta tell you that I got you on speaker, say hi every body."

Everyone said their hello's and we miss you's before I got back to the matter at hand.

"OK so today at Deon's game one of the other player's wives came over to me and told me that she was starting a new perfume line. And guess what?"

"She gave you a free bottle," Aunt Lucy joked.

"No," I laughed. "She wants Violet to be the model for the advertising of it."

"Oh really?"

"Yup. We haven't finalized anything yet because I had to see if Violet wanted to do it or not," I said.

"Well I know her little cute behind didn't say no," Aunt Lucinda joked.

"Aww man Aunt Lucy you go jokes too?" Violet said.

"Oh girl you know it's true," replied Aunt Lucy. "But seriously, I'm proud of you and you definitely have my blessing. As long as you are doing something positive then I am all for it."

"Thank you," Violet said.

"OK. Well Aunt Lucy we're gonna let you go, you have work to do up in that kitchen and we don't want to interrupt. I will call you and let you know how everything goes once I sit down and really talk with this lady, I said.

"Because if she ain't talking right then we're gonna have to take our business else where," Deon butted in.

"Oh I know that's right," Aunt Lucy chuckled.

Everyone said their goodbyes and talk to you laters before I ended the call. I was ecstatic. I wanted Violet to take advantage of every opportunity that she was given. I wanted to instill that go getter attitude within in her early. I was slowly but surely building my family brand.

"Well let's make a toast," I said switching Summer over to my left knee, raising my glass. "To Violet, and her new business venture. Lets support her, and lets make sure that we stay humble and grounded as always. To Violet."

"To Violet," everybody said in unison clanking our glasses together.

Yup. Things were definitely going great.

CHAPTER 13: Youth

Needless to say, the meeting with Tori went excellent. Well almost excellent besides the fact that every time she got a chance she was bragging about LeVelle. Some people just don't know how to chill out sometimes. Everything doesn't have to be a show. But aside from that, it was good. I made made sure that I had my attorney on deck, and Tori's attorney was speaking all the right languages. The deal that Tori offered Violet was beautiful. We would've been crazy to refuse. Five hundred fifty thousand dollars flat just to get her to sign on. Plus a thirty five percent royalty every time a commercial was shown. The deal was gravy. Spectacular for someone who had no modeling experience. So we signed on the dotted line. It was on now. I had this assumption in my head that this perfume line was something small, but boy was I wrong. Tori had paired up with Neiman Marcus, and her perfume line was exclusive to them. In other words, you can only get it from Neiman Marcus stores. That's it. Plus, not only was Tori the wife of a football player, she was also an heiress. Her great grand parents were the owners of the Brexton hotels. Long story short, she had plenty of money backing this business venture. Knowing this, I was going to make sure that we did it right. As soon as I got home I got on the phone and called Rochelle.
"Hey Ro," I greeted her.
"Hey Boop, how did the meeting go?" she asked.
" Five hundred fifty stacks," is all I said.
"What? For her first deal? Are you kidding me?"
"Nope. Dead serious. Plus royalties."
"Well got damn! V made out!"
"Yes. Truly a blessing. So look. I need you to put in a good word for me with that modeling coach in your building," I said.
"Who? Juliet? Girl you not going to be able to put up with that stuck up bitch," Rochelle replied.
"Oh goodness Ro why the lady gotta be all that?"
"Because that's what she is I'm telling you what I know."
"I don't care nothing about her character traits Ro. You know Violet is new to this. I need her to be on point. I got a feeling

this is gonna open up a lot more doors for her. She gotta be on her A-game. And that lady turns the ugliest ducklings into swans you feel me?"

"True. I can' argue with that. She is a beast wit' it," Rochelle agreed.

"Ard that's what I'm talkin' bout. So just put in that word for me please," I said.

"Okay I'll say something to her before my class starts today. Hopefully she won't have a class. She be pissed off when you interrupt her lil' funky ass class," Rochelle laughed.

"That's because your dancers probably be stomping all over top of their heads while they downstairs tryna get their model on, I chuckled.

"Whatever," Rochelle laughed. "Talk to you later."

"Ard. Bye."

I thought about how Tori kept talking about LeVelle. It seemed so crazy to me because I knew that everything wasn't as rosy as she tried to portray. I mean come on, not too long before that, I found a girl's number in Deon's phone that was really for LeVelle. I shook my head, because even though she was a little over the top, I still felt kind of bad for her. She had all this money and power, and she still had a husband that ran around on her. And there was a life lesson tied to all this, well really two. You can't put a man on a pedestal, ever. You will wind up looking stupid every time. What I have learned about men is they have a tendency to mess up a good thing. They are never satisfied, and a lot of their actions are based on ego and pride. So while you're over here bragging to everybody about how your man is the best ever and that he can do no wrong, he is over there being the biggest man whore ever just to prove a point to his boys or to make himself feel like a pimp. Then on top of that, no matter how good of a woman you are that does not make you exempt from being cheated on. You can have money, a good career, be beautiful, and can cook better than a chef and he will still step out on you. Women get so wrapped up in this whole you gotta do all the right things to keep your man fantasy. When in reality, you can never do all the right things. That is impossible because nobody is perfect. And even if you give all you can to your man, the fact of the matter is he is gonna do what he wants to do regardless. Your actions don't control what he does, his own actions do. I love Deon, I really do. But you can never sleep on these dudes. Now I'm not saying you have to be a spy or question everything that he does, but you have to keep your eyes and your ears open. Don't get so wrapped up in your man that you forget that at the end of the day, he is still a human being and that your vagina isn't made out of dead presidents. You gotta stay two steps ahead of them, not one but two. Don't sleep on them ladies, don't put nothing past them.

    But anyway after the deal was signed, everything just kept falling in line. The modeling coach that Rochelle knew, well Ms. Juliet is her name, took Violet under her wing and it was a wrap.

"She is a natural. I don't see that in too many girls," Ms. Juliet said in her Russian accent after Violet's first class was over.

    With every class she got better and better. I mean from couture poses, to ripping the runway, Violet was definitely ready for the big leagues. Now it was time for the real test. Violet and I had to fly to LA for her first photo shoot for "Youth" the fragrance. I don't know who was more nervous, her or me.

"I'm OK Rosie. You're the one sweating," she said to me before she got in front of the camera.

"Are you sure?" I asked her for like the twelfth time.

"Yes, I'm fine. I got this," she said with confidence.

    True to what she said, she was fine. As a matter of fact she was excellent. She was so fluid in her movements, and the photographers didn't have to give her any direction at all. Violet breezed through that shoot like she had been modeling for years. Proud was a complete understatement, and I couldn't wait to call Aunt Lucinda and tell her how good Violet did.

"Well praise God," said Aunt Lucy. "But make sure you keep her grounded. Make sure she knows that this didn't come from her, but from God. You of all people know what this world will do to you. Just please keep her grounded."

I knew that this was going to be a good move for her, I felt it and I went with my gut. Thank God she was with it, because if she wasn't we would've missed that boat for sure. After the shoot was done, I took Violet out to dinner for a little celebration with just the two of us.

"You did really good today, I'm proud of you," I told Violet.

"Thank you," she said blushing.

"So how does it feel to be a model?"

"I'm not really a model Rosie I only did one shoot."

"So, and what does that mean? You have signed yourself to a major deal. This is your first shoot, but trust me there will be more if this is really what you want to do."

"Yeah I do. I never thought that modeling could be so fun. Plus I never thought of myself as a model chic."

"I really don't know why V. You have slimmed out really nicely, and you have a beautiful face. Plus you have the height. All you needed was a little guidance that's all," I said to Violet. "But look, it's one thing that I have to tell you. I want you to keep this with you for the rest of your life. Remain humble. Never forget where you came from. No matter how much fame and fortune you acquire, none of that really matters. Because when you leave this earth you can't take none of it with you. Sure it's fun to have all that stuff, but it doesn't define who you are as a person. Your character does. Remember that."

"Got it," Violet responded.

"So, now that we are having a discussion about your career, there is something that I need to talk to you about," I said.

"OK..."

"You have a choice. I can get you some interviews with some modeling agencies so we can try to get one of them to represent you. They would be booking all your work, and they would be paying you. Or, I can manage you. If I manage you, I will be booking all your work, and I will get a percentage of what you make from every gig that you get. Now, you don't have to make a decision right this second, and it's up to you what you want to do. Either way I am going to support you."

"I want you to be my manger," Violet said, chewing her asparagus.

"Violet you have time to think about it, you don't have to make a decision right this second," I said.

"I know. But what is it to think about? You are my sister, and I would trust you with my career before I would trust anybody else."

"OK, but you know this is my first time doing this and modeling agencies are more experienced."

"Like I said Rosie, I trust you. You made this happen, so I trust you. We're gonna make this money together."

"No V. It was God. He put us in the right place at the right time."

"True. But you could've told Ms. Tori no, especially after all the bad stuff I've been doing. But you didn't, you took a chance with me. You are my partner. You remember that night when we left Baltimore?"

"Yea, I could never forget it," I replied.

"You've been protecting me since back then. I told you I was scared, but you made it OK. And even now, you are making it OK. You came and got me from Virginia when I was too stupid to see what I was worth. You brought me into this awesome career. You show me everyday how to be a good woman. And I don't know if I told you before, but thank you."

  In life, we all have that moment when we come to ourselves. It had taken me to get into my twenties and to have life beat me down before I came to myself. And here she was seventeen years old, having her moment already.

"Your welcome," I said.

CHAPTER 14: I Don't Like Andrew

At first I thought I was dreaming, then I realized that I was awake. It was bad enough that I had trouble sleeping in hotels as it is. Ever since I had gotten myself together, trying to sleep in a hotel was a difficult task. Maybe it was because it reminded me of when I used to get high, maybe it reminded me of when I had no place to stay, or maybe I reminded me of when I was in and out of the rooms sleeping with men for money. So when I finally did drift off into dreamland in a hotel room, I was severely aggravated if I was awakened prematurely.

"Why do you keep hanging up on me? I'm trying to talk but you won't listen! But I love you.... You said that you loved me too, now you're gonna do this?" I heard through the wall.

It was way too late for Violet to be up on the phone arguing with that idiot. She had a shoot at seven, and it was for a very big deal. Since she had been seen on the "Youth" ad, Violet had signed two more deals. It was already two o'clock in the morning. I rolled over and tried to ignore her conversation, but I couldn't. The conversation was way too loud and annoying.

"But I'm out here working that's all! What? You want me to just quit? No don't hang up. Please don't hang up," I heard her whine.

So I rolled out of bed and walked through the adjoining door over to Violet's room to see what was going on. She was sitting on he edge of the bed with her head down. I saw a tear drop from underneath her.

"What's going on?" I inquired.

"Nothing," she lied.

"Come on now. Obviously something is bothering you or you wouldn't be crying."

"Andrew... he just acts so stupid sometimes."

"That's because he is stupid."

"Rosie please don't-"

"Okay, okay. But listen you better stop worrying so much about him and focus more on you. You have a lot going for yourself, don't throw it all away chasing behind him," I advised.
"But I love him, you just don't understand," Violet whined.
"I don't understand? Girl please you just don't know how many men I have loved. But let me tell you something. Love shouldn't hold you back from succeeding and doing great things. If a man really loves you, then he will have no problem seeing you succeed."
"He just keeps saying that I'm out here messing with somebody and I'm not."
"Well if you know you're not then why do you continue to go back and forth with him about it? Violet he is only saying that because he is insecure. He might even be a little jealous of your success. Don't let that sway you from focusing on your career. I'm telling you what I know. If a man loves you then he is going to support you no matter what," I said. "Now I'm going back to bed. Please get some sleep because you know you are not a morning person and we need to be on time for this shoot. You are going to have some massive bags under your eyes if you don't get some rest."
"OK," Violet responded.
"A man needs to like you a little more than you like him. If you show a man that you are head over heels and that he is your almighty then you are in trouble big time. A man will play on that power. Remember that."

   The next morning, Violet was grumpy just as I had expected. That's what happens when you stay up all night arguing with your insecure boyfriend about a bunch of nothing. But I gotta give it to her, once we arrived at the location and she started getting her hair and makeup done she was in her zone. My baby sister was developing a sense of professionalism and I couldn't be prouder. After getting into wardrobe, she got in front of that camera and she killed it! Violet was growing into a beautiful young lady right before my eyes. At that moment I really wished that our Mama was alive to witness it all. Tears welled up in my eyes. A mixture of joy and sadness I believe. Violet was done with her first look, and she walked over to me.

"How did I do?" she asked with a smile.

"Very good," I said.

"What's wrong? Why are your eyes watery?" Violet probed.

"Oh... Nothing's wrong. Just a little tired that's all," I lied.

"Oh... Well you want me to get you some coffee?"

"No I'm fine V. You just go get ready for your second look. I'm good."

I definitely couldn't bring up Mama and make Violet sad too. In certain situations you have to suck it up and be strong, especially if you have someone looking up to you for strength. Being a big sister is tough, especially when your Mama has gone on home... But that's life. You are born and you die. The tough part about it is you never know when it's your time to go, and when and how you go affects the people who love you in a major way. I kept trying to shake the feeling all day, but it was no use. Every now and then you have to just let your feelings flow. It's not possible to keep up a strong front one hundred percent of the time. So I watched Violet do work her second look, and I mean she was so beautiful. All I could think of was how when she was little she used to ask a million questions and how she always complained about us having to eat greens. Now she was making a way for herself. True I was guiding her a little bit, but she still had to get out there and make it happen. I tried to blink back the tears but it didn't work this time. The tears streamed down my cheeks and I tried to wipe them away but they just kept falling. I walked off of the set and went to the bathroom to try to get myself together. Then I heard a knock on the door.

"Some one's in here," I said.

"Rosie it's me."

Oh crap. It was Violet. I fanned my eyes in attempts to dry them out. Then I grabbed more tissue and patted my eyes.

"Give me one sec V," I said.

"Rosie open the door," Violet said. "I know you're crying, so just open the door."

Damn. I was busted. I hated for a person to see me cry. To me crying was a sign of weakness, and I'd be damned if somebody thought I was weak. I patted my eyes one more time then opened up the door.

"Hey wassup," I said pretending to be fine.

"Are you OK?" Violet asked standing in the door way.

"Yeah I'm good. Let me get out of here so you can use the bathroom," I said.

"I don't have to use it. You miss Mama don't you?"

I clenched my jaw so tight that I thought I would break all my teeth. Now why would she ask me that? A tear dropped from my eye.

My voice cracked, "yes."

Violet wrapped her arms around me and hugged me tight. Then the tears came like a flood.

"It's OK. I miss her too," she said.

That moment changed the dynamic between Violet and I. I think that before she saw me break down, Violet probably thought that I kind of brushed the memories of Mama to the side, even though it had been times that I had spoke of missing her. She might have heard me say it, but she never felt me say it. There is definitely a difference.

Once we got back home from New York all I wanted to do was kiss my kids and lay up with Deon. It had been an eventful business trip. We shopped and ate and we bonded. The Big Apple had been great, but I missed my babies and I missed my big hunk of a husband. The whole house rested peacefully once Mommy was back home. The next morning I got back to my routine. I fixed a huge breakfast: eggs, sausage, bacon, french toast, grits, and fried potatoes. Then I did my housework, which consisted of cleaning the house top to bottom and doing the the laundry. After I was done I took another shower, then went to my room to get some rest while Deon was downstairs playing with the kids.

Violet had been in bed all day, and that wasn't normal for her on a Saturday. Usually when she was in town she would be running the streets with her friends or somewhere cuddled

up with that pickle head boyfriend of hers. But not today. She laid in bed and did absolutely nothing. She didn't even get up to eat. I just thought that maybe she had another argument with Andrew and that she was having a little twenty four hour teenage depression, so I just let her have some time to herself.
"Rosie, come help me please!" I heard Violet screaming in pain from down the hall. I ran down the hall to see what was wrong, I had never heard Violet sound like that before. Once I got in her room, she was laying on the floor in the fetal position.
"What's wrong?" I said as I knelt down trying to help her in any way that I could.
"It's my stomach. My stomach is hurting so bad," Violet cried.
"Did you eat something bad?"
"No. I don't know it just hurts," she continued to cry.
"Deon! Deon!" I screamed for my husband.

   I could hear Deon running up the stairs. He ran into the room with Summer in his arms.
"What's going on?" he asked.
"Violet is in pain she said her stomach is hurting. She can't walk. I need to get her to the hospital, she doesn't want to go in an ambulance. I-"
   Before I could finish talking Deon had sat Summer on the bed and scooped Violet off of the floor. He ran down the steps with her and out of the front door. I picked Summer up and ran behind him. When I got outside Deon already had Violet laying across the back seat of my car.
"Here take Summer," I said to him. " I don't want to drag all the kids to the hospital, so you just stay here with them. I'll call you from the hospital and keep you posted."
"Are you sure you don't want us to go?" Deon asked.
"Yeah, I'm sure. I'll call you in a little bit."
   I got in the driver seat, started up the car, and sped off down the street. I had to get Violet to the hospital. Something wasn't right with her, I could tell that this wasn't an act. In my mind I was going over all the possibilities. Appendicitis, pancreatitis, ectopic pregnancy, I mean it could have been anything.

"Lord please help my sister, please heal her body," I thought.

Once we got to the hospital, I pulled up to the entrance of the emergency room and put the car in park. I ran in and got a wheel chair for Violet and brought it outside to the car. Once I got her out of the car and into the wheel chair, I took her inside. After registering with the nurse at the front desk and having Violet's vital signs taken, we were taken straight to a room. Her temperature was 103.2. I was terrified a what might be going on with her. Once I got her in the bed I left for a minute to park my car in the parking garage. I damn sure didn't want to get towed for parking in the fire lane. I would've been pissed. I went back into the hospital after I got my vehicle situated. Violet looked so helpless. I felt so bad for her. As soon as I came back in, a nurse came in to put an IV in. I was so squeamish when it came to needles and blood. Violet took it like a champ though.

I sat in the room with V scared to death. I was no good at keeping calm. I was easily panicked, and to see my little sister in so much pain broke my heart. The nurse finally gave her some pain medication and she fell asleep. I was a nervous wreck. What if she was severely ill? What if she needed some type of surgery? Lord knows I was beside myself. After about an hour V woke up and I was still sitting there right by her side.
"Do you feel any better?" I asked her.
"Yeah a little. The pain medicine is working I guess," she responded.
"OK. Well now we just have to wait for the test results to come back."
"Rosie?"
"Yes."
"I'm scared."

Oh Lord, if she only knew. I think I was more scared for her than she was for herself. But being scared wasn't going to change a thing, prayer would though. So I told her the only thing that I knew could take away her fear.,
"I know. But that is a normal response when you are facing something that you can not control. But if you have faith in

God, then he can work it out for you. Trust me, I know. He helped me when I didn't even acknowledge who He was. He kept His hand over me when I was in situations that could've killed me. So I know you will be fine. Whatever it is, we will get through it. No matter what it is I'm going to be here."
"OK," Violet said.

We sat in the room for another two hours before the doctor actually came in to tell us what was going on. I was so happy to see his face because I was tired of sitting and wondering. I needed to know what was the problem with my little sister.
"OK. So all the test results came back normal except for one. You have what we refer to as a Pelvic Inflammatory Disease, or what is also known as a P.I.D."
"What is that?" Violet asked.
"Well it's and infection of the pelvis, the uterine lining, fallopian tubes, or ovaries. In your case there is an infection of your ovaries. This happens when bacteria enters your vagina, and then travels upward into the reproductive organs. The bacteria that has caused your infection is the bacteria that causes chlamydia," Dr. Morgan said.
"Huh?"
I butted in, "That damn boy gave you chlamydia and you have had it so long that it has moved up to your ovaries. And the fact that you don't even understand what this doctor is saying to you tells me that you shouldn't even be having sex in the first place."

Violet sat on the bed in silence. Her mind was in about a million different places, I could tell that just by the look on her face. I was so disappointed in her.
"So how long will she have to be on the antibiotics to clear it up?" I asked.
"If this were a mild case, we would give her a shot of antibiotics and then send her home with a prescription to take for a week or two. But being that she has a more severe case, she is going to have to stay here for a few days. We need to keep her under close observation to make sure that fever stays

down, and just to monitor her. We will give her antibiotics through her IV while she is here, and then we will send her home with a prescription as well. She will have to follow up with her gynecologist to make sure everything has cleared up once she finishes her medication."

I took a deep breath and shook my head. I looked over at Violet. She wouldn't look at me. She just ought to be ashamed.

"OK. Dr. Morgan. Thank you so much," I said. "Will I be able to stay with her?"

"Sure. We're going to move her up to her room shortly."

"OK. Thanks again," I said.

Dr. Morgan nodded his head and left the room. I was glad because I was ready to light into Violet's ass! I could not believe this! But I should've known something was up when she was screaming bloody murder during the pap smear that they had given her after they had drawn her blood. I looked at her and I shook my head.

"Here I am about to lose my mind because you are acting like you are dying, and all this is because you keep sleeping with that stupid ass boy with the filthy penis? Come on now Violet wake the hell up please! Is this gonna be enough for you to leave him alone? He don't care nothing about you as you can see! Because if he did, then he would at least have the decency to protect himself when he is out in these streets hoeing around!"

"Rosie please don't do this. Please. I know that I gotta break up with him. I know that. I will handle it. Just please don't come at me with the I told you so stuff. I am so hurt right now, I can't take you being mad with me. I really didn't know," Violet said.

I looked at the pain in her eyes and I couldn't even fuss at her anymore. This just took me back to when I was a teenager in love. I accepted so much foolishness from Franko, but you still couldn't tell me that the sun didn't rise and set in his pants. I heard what her mouth said, but I knew that this wasn't it. This definitely wasn't over yet. So I took off the hat of guardian and put on the the hat of the understanding big sister.

"I'm sorry. I just want the best for you Violet and this is not the best. You have compromised your health. Do you realize that this could have easily been H.I.V or A.I.D.S.?"

Violet hung her head and nodded. I let out a deep sigh and held her in my arms. I knew that this had to be hard for her. She had to find out that this dude that she loved was cheating on her, and she had to find out by being hospitalized because he had passed something on to her. Not to mention she was probably embarrassed as hell. If only she had listened to me. If only she had listened. That's when I was hit with another lesson. As a parent or older sibling you try your best to shield your loved ones from the hurt and pain that you once experienced. You try to warn them. You drill it into their heads over and over again. But you can talk until you are blue in the face, the fact of the matter is a lot of the time experience is the best teacher. You will never know how much something hurts until you actually feel that hurt first hand for yourself. It just saddened me that she had to figure it out like this. Suddenly I went from hurt to angry. The thought of the little chump of a nigga made my skin crawl. His little nasty ass really burned my sister. He better not ever let me see him in the street because I was gon' sure 'nough put my little cute ass foot, right up his chlamydia infected ass. Just as I was in my thoughts of how I was gonna strangle that clown Violet spoke.

"Rosie?"

"Yes."

"Please don't tell nobody about this. Especially Aunt Lucinda," she sniffled.

"OK. I won't," I said.

CHAPTER 15: It's A Celebration

Life was really a whirlwind at this point. My daycare center was doing numbers in the city, and I had just started up my new business geared toward child care services for celebrities. These child care providers are what we refer to as nannies. And to top it all off, I was finally ready to get into my dream, and that was being the owner of my own shoe line! Everything was definitely falling right into place.

But that wasn't even what I was the most excited about. I was so proud of Violet. She had done a complete turn around from when I had gotten her from Virginia seven months ago. She was doing excellent in school, and she was tearing the modeling world apart. I knew she had it in her. All it took was some hard work and discipline. The only thing that she was still doing that I didn't approve of was still dealing with that damn Andrew, and at this point I was tired of fighting with her about him. I felt like he wasn't going to be around too much longer anyway. I know some girls grow up to be women and marry the dude that they were so in love with during their teenage years. But there were also a lot of them that didn't, and I felt it deep down in my spirit that Andrew wasn't going to last. I just continued to pray that day would be sooner than later.

The modeling opportunity for the "Youth" fragrance line had opened up so many doors for Violet. She was traveling all over the world for paid gigs, and was still staying up on her school work. I had a tutor with her while she was away, and I made sure that she did all her assignments and that they were turned in as soon as she got back in town from work. I mean she was really doing the damn thing. So I was not surprised when I got a call from some very important people at Teen Vogue. They wanted Violet to be on the cover! I was stoked! This was such a wonderful opportunity! V was definitely in the big leagues now. Since she had been doing such a good job with everything that she had going on, I thought that it would be a good idea to give her a party. The party was to celebrate her making the cover of Teen Vogue. I just wanted to show her that when you did great things in my household, then I would treat you accordingly. That's how I raised my kids. I you did good, you were rewarded. If you didn't do good then you got the necessities, and that was it. That's why everyone in my house were straight A students. Aside from they fact that they were intelligent kids, they applied themselves because they wanted the perks that they knew I was able to provide. Vacations to Hawaii, helicopter rides, etc. Sure we had the means to do those types of things for them just because, but we weren't trying to raise brats. We were trying to teach them to be the best that they could be. That's how I kept them in line. Well not really. They knew not to play with me because they ain't want me to put my foot up their behind, but that's a whole 'nother story.

  So I got on the phone with the ladies over at Exquisite Events, one of the best event planning companies in Baltimore. I had to make this event a night to remember. Violet really deserved it. So when I sat down with the event planners, there was so much to talk about. Color scheme, guest list, menu, time, photographer, venue, etc. Planning a great event was way more than a notion, but I loved having big parties. After everything was in place, I was on pins and needles waiting for the day to arrive. I thought of the perfect lie (if there is a such thing) to tell Violet to get her to the party. I told her we had to go to a red carpet event with Deon, and since she already thought she was a very important person she was ecstatic about going. Hahaha! I couldn't wait to see the look on her face when she walked into that party. I called my aunt and invited her, but she respectfully declined as I knew she would. She was not into the party scene and I totally understood. One of the biggest dilemmas I was having was should I invite Andrew or not. I knew that Violet would love to have him there, but I wouldn't. He would probably nag her all night. I really didn't want to invite him because knowing him, he would be so jealous that she was having something special planned for her, that he might spill the beans about the whole thing. If he was the cause for the surprise being ruined, I would have no choice but to choke him out. So to avoid all that, I decided not to invite him. If he had a problem with it when the time came he would have me to deal with, and I really didn't think that he wanted those type of problems in his life.

So the day of the party had come. It was a Saturday and it was perfect May weather; not too hot, and not a rain cloud in sight. I sent the kids over to my mother in laws house and went on about my day. First stop was to the hair salon to get our hair done, then to the nail salon. We already had our dresses and shoes at the house, so I decided that we could go and have a late lunch to kill some more time. Violet seemed to be enjoying her day, and she was so excited about going to this non existent red carpet event for Deon. She didn't have a clue. As we ate I laughed silently in my head every time she talked about all the celebrities that she was going to meet.

It seemed as if the day just flew by. Before I knew it, the make up artist was leaving our house, and Violet and I were getting dressed. Now it was time to head on out. Just as we had gotten situated in our vehicle my phone rang. It was Deon calling to give me the OK to come.
"We're on our way," I said.

I hung up the phone and looked at Violet. She looked so stunning. She wore a peach gown with a sweetheart neckline, with gold accessories. Her hair was a plum color, about an inch past her shoulders, with bangs that covered her eyelids. She was sure to turn heads when she walked into the party. Once we got there, our driver got out and opened the car door for us. Violet looked kind of disappointed when no one was outside except for security and the photographer.
"Where is everybody?" she asked me.
"They must be inside already, I guess we are a couple minutes late," I fibbed.

We took a couple of pictures on the red carpet, and then we proceeded to the door. My stomach was doing all types of flips, I was so nervous. I just wanted everything to be perfect.
"You go in first," I said.

Violet opened the door and walked in. I could see the enormous crowd from behind her.
"Surprise!" everyone screamed as she walked in the door.
Violet turned around and looked at me with puzzled expression. I pointed to the giant poster of her Teen Vogue cover that was on the wall. She was definitely surprised, mission accomplished.
"Oh! Thank you so much Rosie! Thank you!" she screamed.
Violet hugged me so tight that I thought I might suffocate. I was so happy that she was happy. This event had been pulled off without a hitch. She had no idea that I had been planning it.
"Oh my goodness it looks so beautiful in here!" Violet squealed with excitement. I looked around and realized that the space really did look magnificent. Purple was Violet's favorite color, so I decided to go with the royalty theme, which consisted of purple and gold. The tables were covered in gold linens embroidered with purple floral patterns. There were gold chairs with purple velvet seats and the drapes were purple. The centerpieces were enormous vases filled with violets, and draped with crystals. Gold flatware and plates. Gold goblets encrusted with purple jewels. And to top it all off, huge posters of all of Violet's photo shoots all over the walls. I pointed to the top of the winding staircase, where there was an area where all her closest girlfriends were sitting. That was what the event planners delegated as her V.I.P. area. There was another space up there for Rochelle, Deon and I. Violet stood there in awe. Mission accomplished.
"Well go ahead and enjoy yourself," I told her.
So everything was going well and everyone was having a great time. The servers were passing the hors d'oeuvres and they were just as tasty as they were at the tasting. Mini quiches, shrimp cocktail, spring rolls, and crab balls were just a few things that were being served. I spotted Violet looking at her phone then walking toward the front door, so I hurried over to her.
"Where you going?" I asked her.

"Oh I'm just stepping out real quick. Andrew is outside."
"Well tell him to come in, he's more than welcome to come in," I lied.
"I told him that but he said he don't want to. Imma just go out there and talk to him for a few minutes," Violet said.
"OK, but you know you have guests in here. They are here to see you, so don't be long," I told her.
"OK I'm not. I'm only gonna be like five minutes," she reassured me.

   I nodded my head, and she went outside. I prayed for the day that she would finally leave that boy alone. He was a knuckle head in every meaning of the word. And Violet was head over heels for him. I couldn't stand him. But it was no use in me worrying about her so called relationship with him. Worrying wasn't gonna change anything. So I just prayed on a regular basis that a change would come.

   Rochelle walked over to me, and I know she could tell that I wasn't in the right mood that I was supposed to be in. I guess it was my body language. I stood right where I was looking toward the front door with my arms folded and my eyebrows scrunched.
"What's the matter?" Rochelle asked me.
"She went out side to talk to that clown," I said.
"Why didn't he just come in?"
"I don't know. He probably got an attitude because he wasn't invited. But he is such a hater I didn't want to invite him because he probably would've told her about it and ruined the surprise."
"Yea that's true. Well fuck him. Let him stand his dumb ass outside then," Rochelle laughed.
"Yup, that sounds about rite," I responded with a laugh of my own.

   Rochelle went back into the V.I.P. area, but I didn't move from where I was. I still stood there, staring at the door waiting for her to come back in. Everybody was having a good time though. A few people came up to me and told me how nice the party was. I smiled and thanked them for coming.

Then a couple of her girlfriends came up to me and asked where's she was, and that's when I knew that I should go get her. Violet was taking a little too long coming back inside, something in me told me that I should go out there just to check on her. I excused myself and made my way to the door. I'm so glad that I went out to get her when I did. Just as I stepped outside of the venue Andrew was grabbing Violet by her arm. His back was turned so he didn't see me.
"Get off of me," Violet said snatching away.

And with the blink of an eye, he raised his hand and slapped her across her face. Violet stumbled backward. It was cool though, because I was right there to knock the shit right out of him. I swung from behind him hitting him in his left ear making him stagger to the right. I never gave him a chance to get it back right because when he staggered I just kept following up. The next thing I knew Violet had jumped in it too. I mean he was literally out there getting his ass whipped by two females. We got work done. Andrew finally got on his feet and he looked like he was ready for round two. I stood in front of Violet, because I knew it was about to get even uglier.
"What the fuck is going on out here?" I heard Deon say.
"Man fuck you I ain't scared of you. You don't wanna see me," Andrew said as if he could really fight.

I backed away and pulled Violet away because I knew this wasn't going to be pretty at all. I don't know if Andrew was drunk or high off of some type of pill, but he was mighty brave. All I could do was shake my head because I could only imagine what was in store for him. Deon walked toward him and my heart started to beat faster.
"So you like to fight females huh?" Deon asked him.
"Man you need to get your girl in check. She is too fuckin' nosy. That was between me and my girl," Andrew said with his chest stuck out.

Deon hit him with one punch and his whole tune changed.
"Look man.. I don't even wanna fight no more," Andrew said as he picked himself up off of the ground.

"Well then get from 'round here then," Deon said to him.
　　　　Andrew ran to his car and sped off like the coward that he was. Finally he had showed his true colors with no filter.
"Yall OK?" Deon asked.
"Yea," I said.
"Yall were gone for too long, so I had to come and see what was going on. I had a feeling something wasn't right."
"Thank you," Violet cried.
"Aww come one now V. Don't cry. You want me to go to his house?" Deon asked.
　　　　Violet didn't respond. She was hurt and it was no way around it.
 "Just let me talk to her for a minute," I said to my husband.
"Ard," he said.
　　　　Deon went back inside and I knelt down beside Violet. She was sitting on the curb hysterical. I totally understood. But I couldn't let her night end like this.
"Violet baby it's OK. If don't nobody on this earth got you, I got you. As long as I'm here you ain't gotta worry about nothing. If he even thinks about laying a finger on you again I will make sure that he will be taken care of."
"I'm so embarrassed," she cried.
"It's OK. I'm the one that should be embarrassed. I'm a grown woman fighting outside of my little sister's party," I laughed.
"No for real Rosie. You kept telling me and I didn't listen and look at what happened."
"Well that's a part of life V. Sometimes you just don't listen because you just gotta figure it out for yourself. It's OK and it's not the end of the world."
"I was so stupid."
"Love can make you do stupid things. Trust me, I've been there and done that. But it's no sense in beating yourself up about it. Now it's time to learn from your mistakes and move on."
"Yea you're right. It's time for me to leave him in the dust. I got way more important things to be worried about," Violet said.
"That's what I'm talking about," I replied."Now let's go party. It's a celebration remember?"

"Yup," Violet said. " I need some more of them crab balls."
	We laughed and went back inside. Everybody was still having a good time, and Violet went back to enjoying herself as well.
"Everything good?" Rochelle asked.
"Yeah. The devil is finally gone for good," I replied.
"They broke up?"
"Yup. He hit her."
"What? I knew I should've came out there!"
"It's cool. We handled it. Then Deon came out there and knocked him off his feet. Sent him running like a little girl."
"Damn! I told you security should've been outside all night," Rochelle said.
"Yeah, you did. But oh well. Everything happens for a reason. She's good so that's all that matters," I responded.
	The end of the party was approaching, and I had one more trick up my sleeve. I grabbed the microphone and got everyone's attention.
"Excuse me.... Can everyone come outside for a minute please?" I spoke.
	I could see everybody looking around at each other trying to figure out what was going on. I loved to keep folk in suspense. Everyone started to make their was outside, and Violet and I were the last ones to go. All the guests were standing outside looking around when we came out.
"What's going on?" Violet asked me.
"You will see in a minute girl calm down," I chuckled.
	I stood there with a huge grin, because of course, I knew what was in store. I could see headlights coming into the lot. I looked at Violet as her eyes grew larger and larger. And there it was, her big surprise. An all white BMW X3, just for my baby sis. I mean she really did deserve it. She had done all the things that I had asked her to do. She had become a straight A student while traveling for work. She had really become a classy young lady and that's all that I wanted for her. I couldn't ever be content with her being a slouch.

Deon got out of the truck and handed Violet the keys. She jumped up and down and screamed to the top of her lungs. All her guests clapped and cheered at the sight of her new gift.

"Thank yall!" Violet screamed and hugged us.

"No problem. Only the best for those who do their best," Deon said.

After she took about fifty pictures in front of her new ride, everybody went back inside and danced the rest of the night away. Even though their was a minor glitch, Violet's night still turned out perfect.

CHAPTER 16: Rose Pedals and Birthday Betrayal

"A nanny? Have you lost your damn mind?" I asked him.

"No Rosie. But look. You have a lot going on. Especially since you are doing a lot of traveling with V. I think it would be good for you. I really do. Then you wont have to drag the kids out of town every time you have something to do."

"I can't trust nobody with my kids. Nobody will take care of your kids like you do," I said.

"Rosie. Relax. We can interview as many as you want. It's not like if she does something wrong you won't know. All the kids are old enough to tell you what's going on except Deon and Summer. So if something funky is going on you know one of the older ones is gonna tell one of us. Just think about it." Deon said.

"I don't know Deon. I don't know if that's for me."

"So what you're meaning to tell me is that your nannies are good enough to take care of all your clients' children, but not yours?" Deon asked.

"No Deon that's not the point. I'm not uppity. I'm not bougie. I'm from the old school where people take care of their own kids."

"I get what you're saying Rosie. But your are not living the life of somebody from the old school though. You do a lot of traveling and I'm gone a lot too. Having a nanny does not discredit you as a mother. It will just make things a little less complicated for you. That's all I'm saying."

    Deon was right, I did need a little extra help with managing the kids. I was always on the go and sometimes having the kids with me made things a tad bit harder than they would be if I could fly solo. True, his mother helped out a lot too, but I didn't like having to depend on her all the time either. So after a few days of thinking long and hard, I decided to give it a try. We interviewed a few candidates, and ended up deciding on Michelle, a middle aged woman whose nationality was Black and Vietnamese. She had plenty of credentials. I got good reports from all my clients about her, and all the children just adored her. After Deon and I interviewed her we decided that she would be a great person to take care of our children.

So finally it was time to for Michelle to stay with the kids. I was extremely nervous about leaving them, but Deon reassured me that everything would be fine. I had to fly to LA to take care of some things for my shoe line, Rose Pedals. I was really sad to go because not only would I be away from the kids, but I would also be away from Deon during his birthday week. He kept telling me that it was OK, and that he wasn't upset but I still couldn't help but to feel guilty. I already had it in my mind that I was going to have a few things express shipped to him from LA on his birthday, since he would be getting back in town on that day.

I cried like I never went out of town without my kids before. This time was a little different though, I was trusting someone who wasn't family with the most precious things in my life. I made sure to tell the kids that if Michelle did or said anything out of line to call me and let me know. Violet promised to let me know that she would make sure that nothing happened to the kids, so that put me a little more at ease. As soon as I got to my hotel I called and checked on the kids, then I called Deon. After I made my phone calls, it was time to get to work. Meetings, meetings, and more meetings. Looking at sketches, going over marketing plans, and looking a fabric swatches.

Over the next three days it was work and no play. My goal was to see at least one pair produced before I left LA. I needed to see the shoe live and full in the flesh so to speak. I wanted to put my foot inside of them. I wanted to walk in them so that I could know how they would feel to my customers. I wanted them to be perfect, my name was on the line so I had a lot riding on this.

Finally, the day had come for me to see the sample shoe, and I was so excited. It was such a wonderful feeling to see your ideas come to life. After I got out of the meeting I got on the phone and called Deon. I was so excited about the shoe line. God had been placing his favor on me for sure. Who

would've thought that little old me would have so much positive going on in my life? A successful day care, nanny services, and managing the hottest model in the game right now. And now this! Rose Pedals was really under way. Wow. When I was on the streets just existing, just doing anything that I was big and bad enough to do... I never thought that I would be where I was in that very moment. The girl who got pregnant at the age of sixteen had grown to be a woman that was focusing on all things positive. That's when I was hit with another life lesson. Never count anyone out. God can use anyone that he chooses to. You never know what a person can turn out to be. Even the lowliest individual can grow to be someone spectacular if they are given a chance. My thoughts were broken by the sound of Deon's voice.
"Hello?"
"So how is my birthday boy doing?" I asked.
"Hey baby I'm good. Thanks for the gifts. They are really nice," Deon answered.
"Your welcome. Anything for my hubby," I responded.
"How did everything go today?" he asked.
"Oh my goodness Deon everything went so good! I saw the first two shoes and they are bad! I can't wait until the whole line drops! I am just so grateful for everything that I have going on right now," I said.
"Well if you are happy, then I'm happy. So what are you about to get into?"
"I'm starving, so I'm gonna go get some lunch. Then I'm gonna go back to the hotel and get some rest. I have one more meeting later on this evening and I gotta catch my flight at eight in the morning tomorrow. Where are the kids?
"Out in the pool with Michelle."
"Oh OK. Well I wish I could be there with you to celebrate your birthday, I feel so bad that I'm away."
"Babe I told you it's OK. You'll be back tomorrow so we can celebrate then it's not a big deal. I know if you could be here then you would. I ain't mad because I know you're out there

getting that money. That's strong black business woman money!" Deon joked.

"And don't you ever forget it," I laughed. "I miss you so much Deon."

"I miss you too."

"Oh! Let Michelle know that her check will be deposited into her account in the morning," I said.

"Oh ard, cool. Imma let her know when she's done playing with the kids."

"Well she knows she can go since you're home now right?" I asked.

"Yea, I told her. But the kids wanted her to stay a little while longer. They were playing Marco Polo," Deon chuckled.

"Them kids always gotta play a damn game no matter what they're doing. Crazy ass kids," I remarked.

"Yeah they got too much energy for me, and I play sports..."

"Well ard babe. Let me get out of here and get some lunch and rest my eyes before I have to go to this meeting at six. I love you, and Happy Birthday again baby," I said.

"Thanks Rosie. I love you too."

  I missed my family so much. Don't get me wrong, I loved being a business woman but I hated being away from my husband and children. Deon sounded like he really missed me too. So while I was a lunch, I got on the phone and booked a red eye to Baltimore for that night. I was going to surprise my baby. I hated sleeping alone in those lonely hotels. I was gonna sleep in my bed with my husband tonight. I was so excited to see him. I had only been away four days, but it seemed eternity. And since it was off season and Deon was home a lot more, I wanted spend as much time with him as possible. After lunch, I went back to the hotel and packed my luggage. After that I took a nap. I knew that once I got back in town I was going to roll around in the sheets with Deon, so I needed to be well rested.

  I boarded my flight at ten that night, and I was back in Baltimore at around three thirty the next morning. I hopped in a cab and finally I was there. Home sweet home. When I pulled up in the driveway I was surprised to see Michelle's car still there. I could have sworn Deon said that she was on her way out the door when I had talked to him earlier that day. Whatever. I rolled my luggage up the walkway and unlocked the front door. I flicked on the light switch and disarmed the alarm. I left my luggage at the door and walked through the dining area. Something wasn't right I could feel it. Ladies the one thing that God blessed us with that a man doesn't have, is women's intuition. Yes it is real, so make sure you use it. If you have that little voice in your head telling you that something isn't right, then something isn't right! Anyway, in my peripheral view I saw that the lamp in the sun parlor was on, so I went to go turn it off. When I stepped into the door way I was appalled. Never in a million years did I think that I would come home to this. I had definitely been blind sided.

    I stood in the door way and looked at them in awe. There they were, the nanny and my husband all cuddled up in the sun parlor, on my eleven thousand dollar sofa. Champagne bottles all over the floor. They were so drunk that they didn't even hear me coming in. The nerve of those two. But I had something up my sleeve for these two sleeping beauties. I crept to the kitchen and turned the cold water on. I filled up a pitcher with ice, then added some cold water to it. Then I went back into the sun parlor, stood over the two freaky little fuckers... THEN I DUMPED THE WHOLE PITCHER RIGHT ON THIER TRIFLING ASS FACES! They looked like they were drowning... Wooo hooo I've never seen two black people move so fast! Hahahahahahahahaha! Every time I think about it I get tickled pink.

    And there it was, life lesson number.... Well I don't even know what number it was. I've had so many life lessons that I have lost count. But anyway, you can't trust no woman around your man, NO WOMAN. I had gotten so wound up in making sure that she was doing right by my kids, that I had totally let my guard down about her being alone with Deon. Then I was hit with another life lesson. Dag, back to back.... if he cheats with you, he will cheat on you, and that's real talk. I was no different than Trina. I didn't doubt that he loved me, because I knew that he did. But just as I had been a temptation for him with Trina, the nanny was a temptation for him with me. And then I continued to think. I couldn't even be mad at her... (but she still was gonna get it) You know why? Because she saw her shot and she took it. She was no friend of mine, therefore she had no loyalty to me. Who wouldn't want to get in bed with a football player that made millions of dollars?

Michelle jumped up scrambling for her clothes. I hurled chunks of ice at her as she tried to get her clothes on. Deon was doing the same.

"Naw bitch you wanted to be naked, so stay your little stankin' ass naked then! Get the fuck out my house before I snatch every piece of that dry ass weave out of your bobble ass head!" I screamed.

Michelle ran out of the house in her panties with her clothes in her hands, dropping her shoes on her way out the door. I picked up one of her shoes and threw it at her, bopping her in the back of the head.

"There goes your cheap ass shoe bitch! You ain't getting the other one! You better hop home! And you can forget about that check because I ain't depositing shit! You should've got some money from him after you got finished being a hoe!" I screamed at her as she continued to run to her car.

I ran back in the house with her other shoe in my hand and started beating the brakes off of Deon with it. I was like a wild bull in that sun parlor. Deon finally pinned me up against the wall. I tried my best to get from under his grasp but he was just too strong.

"Get off of me! Get out of my house! Get out! I hate you!" I screamed.

"Rosie just calm down, you are gonna wake the kids up," he said to me.

"Oh so now you're so worried about the kids? But you were just in here fucking the same bitch that was supposed to be taking care of the kids while I was gone? This shit was all your idea! Get a nanny you said.. It will be fine you said.."

"I know I was wrong, but-"

"Nigga it aint no but! The only but here is the butt you were digging up in all night and it wasn't mine! Now you go ahead and chase behind her, go ahead! I wanna see how long this is gonna last."
"But I don't love her, I love you Rosie. You know that."
"I also know that you slept with the Nanny when you thought that I was still out of town. Obviously love didn't mean anything to you when you were on the sofa with that skank. But listen it's cool. I'm not gonna make this hard for you at all. Just pack your shit up and go. You can get Summer whenever you want, and I will let you know when I want to keep Deon and Deonte'. We can work out how much money you're gonna give me per month once I cool off a little bit," I said.

Deon shook his head and let me go. He walked out of the sun parlor and went upstairs. I followed behind him and stood in the bedroom door way watching him pack a few things up. I tried to fight back the tears but it was too hard not to cry. I had tried so hard to be a good wife, a faithful wife. I had stood by him through everything. The whole ordeal with Baby Deon, his lunatic of a mother, Trina and her spiteful ass, the groupies, him being gone all the time... I had endured it all. And this was the thanks I get? While I'm out of town handling business, making sure that I bring more bread to the table he decided that he was so horny that he was just going to sleep with the nanny? Oh hell no. As much as I didn't want him to leave, I couldn't let him stay. He was too wrong for this. Deon put on his clothes and shoes. Then he walked over to the bed and reached for baby Deon.

"You're not taking him out of here this time of night. Come back and get him later on. I'll have have his stuff ready when you get here."

Deon looked at me and nodded his head. He grabbed his suitcase and walked toward me.
"I love you," he said. "Please don't make me leave."
"Get out. And leave my key," I said with tears streaming down my face.

Deon left the house and I got in bed with Summer and Baby Deon. I cried myself to sleep.

CHAPTER 17: Attempting to Carry On

The next few days were hard as hell. Every time I walked past the sun parlor I teared up. It still felt unreal to me, I still couldn't shake that awful sting of betrayal. About a week after the incident happened I got a call from Deon's mother. The way that I was feeling about her son made me feel a little salty when I saw her number pop up on my caller ID, but I still answered. Something deep inside me wanted her to try to talk slick. Since I was so pissed with Deon I wanted to beef with his mother too. I was mad at the world literally.

"Hello," I answered.
"Hey Rosie," she said.
"Hi," I said.
"Well I was just calling to check on you, that's all."
"Oh OK."
"Oh, and another thing... Since school is out, I wanted to know if I could get the kids for a few weeks," Ms. Bonita said.
"Um well I guess you can get Summer. Sure," I replied.
"What about Miracle and Franko?" she asked.
"I don't want you or your son to think that I'm trying to pawn my kids off on yall. That's OK. They can stay home."
"Listen Rose. I get it. I get that you are upset with Deon. You have every right to be. But I don't have anything to do with that. What he did was what he did due to his own stupidity. Now you know that I love all of those children the same. I don't care if they are not my blood they are still my grand children. I'm trying to take some of the load off of you for a little while so you can get your thoughts together. Trust me I have been there. You don't have to try to battle with me. I am going to be there for you and those kids regardless of what you and Deon are going through."

I didn't say a word. Why did she have to be such a nice person? It was too damn hard to be mean to someone who was so loving and caring. This phone call also convinced me even more that I was changing for the better. A few years prior I would've invited her to kiss my ass and some more stuff even though she was just trying to be there for me.

"Hello?"

"Yes, I'm still here Ms. Bonita," I said. "I apologize for coming off the way that I did. You can get them if you want."

"It's OK. I understand. I'll come get them tomorrow. Is that OK?"

"Yes. Thank you," I said.

"No problem," Ms. Bonita responded.

Once Ms. Bonita came to get the kids, I was left with my thoughts. I didn't have taking care of them to preoccupy my mind anymore. So I called Rochelle over for a girls night in with some wine and food, just to try to clear my head.

"I'm glad you called me over, I didn't know what was going on with you since you weren't answering my calls," Rochelle said as she sat down on my bed.

"Girl I know. My bad, I didn't want to talk to anybody really. I felt kind of embarrassed about the whole thing," I replied.

"Embarrassed? For what?"

"Because here I am traveling trying to take care of business, and my supposed to be husband is laying up in the sun parlor, with the Nanny while my kids are sleep. Everybody expects my life to be so perfect, and it's really not. I haven't even told my Aunt yet, I can't bring myself to tell her about another failed relationship."

"First of all, I don't expect your life to be perfect. I am your friend. I don't care if you are up or if you are down because I'm gonna be your friend regardless. I'm not gonna look at you no different because of something your husband did. That was his fault not yours. I'm gonna always be here for you, if you ain't figure that out by now girl," responded Rochelle.

"Thanks," I said.

"No problem. I don't like to see you all down and out. You got too much going for yourself right now. It'll be OK. Yall will be back together, you just need to cool off."

"Naw I don't see that happening. I'm done," I said.

"Yea right girl that's your husband. And both you and I know men are fuck ups, they don't know what's good til it's gone," Rochelle said.

"Yeah, but how can I ever trust him again? I can't even walk past the sun parlor without that damn couch looking like it got all that stank hoe's germs all over it."

"Well get rid of it."

"Huh?"

"Get rid of the couch. If it irritates you that bad, get rid of it and get a new one. It's that simple," Rochelle replied.

"That's crazy because I never thought of that," I said.

"I know, you were too busy being depressed. I know that's your husband and all, and I know it hurts. I mean I would think you were crazy if that didn't faze you, but you can't let a man determine your happiness Rose, you know that. You better take this time to build your business and get some more money, don't waste time sitting around moping. I bet he ain't laying around crying all day," said Rochelle.

"That's true. I just can't believe that he would betray me like that."

"I know, but the thing about betrayal is it never comes from your enemy, so of course it's gonna hurt," replied Rochelle. "You have been through way worse things than this, girl this ain't nothing."

"I know right.. But wassup with the Asian community? Why they always stealing my men?"

"Why you gotta be so stupid?" Rochelle roared in laughter.

"I'm for real! They be coming for me hard! First Chu now Michelle," I laughed. "And I can't get away from them damn Michelle's either. First Marlon's crazy ass wife, now this home wrecker. Oh my goodness, I'm getting all my stuff back. Karma is real."

    Rochelle and I laughed and talked for hours. It felt good to finally let all of that off of my chest, and to know that she wasn't judging me. True friends don't judge, period. They don't take your business and spread it to someone else. And they don't paint a negative picture of you to anyone else. True friends don't hold you to unrealistic expectations either. They don't expect to talk to you every day or for you to be up under them twenty four seven. True friends don't label you as disloyal

when you decide that you want to do something on your own or you take some time to work on you. A true friend never feels threatened by your success and they don't get jealous either. They congratulate you and they always know that when you get on, your gonna make sure that they will to. Rochelle was my true friend, and I trusted her with my life. She was never fake or phoney and she never was around because of what I had. True friends are really hard to come by, especially in this day and age. That's why I never took our friendship for granted.
"Well on a more serious note, I've been thinking about something else here lately," I said breaking up the jolly tone in the room.
"What? Is it bad?" Rochelle asked after gulping down the rest of her wine.
"I mean.. I don't think so," I replied.
"OK, so spill it," Rochelle requested.
"I've been thinking about trying to find my father."
"For real?"
"Yeah I'm for real. It's been on my mind heavy lately. But I don't know."
"Well what's not to know?" inquired Rochelle.
"Like what's the point? My mother didn't want me to know who he was for a reason obviously, so maybe it's just not meant for me to know," I answered.
"I hear what you're saying, but I feel like everybody deserves to know who their parents are, whether they're a good person or a bad person. You at least deserve to know. I mean once you find out then you can decide whether you want to carry on with it. I mean that's just my opinion."
" But then where do I start?"
"Now that I can't tell you.... Look it up on Google. You know you can find anything out on Google. I guess you should put in how to find a lost parent or something like that. I'm pretty sure it'll give you some options."
"I don't know... I guess I'll just sleep on it," I said to Rochelle.
Who Are You?

After all this time all I really want to really know is, who are you?
Do you know about me?
Do I look like you?
Do I have your teeth?
Am I outspoken like you?
Did you love my Mama?
Or was it a one night stand?
Did you really want me?
Was a baby girl a part of your plans?
Do I laugh like you?
What is your name?
Why didn't you look for me?
Who am I really?
Until I know who you are
I don't think that I will know that fully.
How could a man just walk away from something that is his?
Don't you feel incomplete without me?
Or do I even matter to you?
Because in some strange way, you matter to me?
I mean really
Who are you?
Are you dark?
Are you light?
Are you short?
Are you tall?
Do you even care that I exist at all?
Because you weren't there when I scraped my knee.
You weren't there when he took my innocence from me.
You didn't help out when I needed new shoes.
So can you please tell me where were you?
But what I really want to know is, who are you?

CHAPTER 18: Down Pour

After I stopped by the daycare, I laid across the sofa watching TV for the majority of the day. None of Elaina's children had been there in over a week. I found that to be kind of odd, since their attendance had drastically improved. My gut told me that something just wasn't right, so I decided to stop past her house to check on them. I knew that she wouldn't be thrilled to see me, but I didn't care. I knocked on her door and I got no answer. I banged for about ten minutes and I still got no answer. As I was about to leave the next door neighbor came outside.
"Hi," I said. "Have you seen Elaina?"
"Yea last week. She got evicted I think," the neighbor said.
"Really?"
"Yea I think so."

I walked off the porch in defeat. Seeing them at the daycare at least let me know that they were doing OK. Now I had no way to tell. I wondered where they were, and if they had a place to stay. Damn it's hard out here. So this in combination with the Deon stuff wasn't helping me come of my funk. I had some good days, but I still had some that weren't so good. Violet came in at about nine thirty talking my head off about how her and her home girls were planning a trip to Miami for winter break. For the life of me I couldn't understand why they were planning a trip for winter break when summer break wasn't even over, but whatever. I reminded her that she may have to work during the break, so maybe she should just plan for her friends to fly with her to where ever she was working, and they could find something to do there. She agreed that my idea made sense and then went up to her room to call them up and tell them the new plan. That Violet was a real trip. I wondered what she thought she was going to be doing in Miami anyway. She wasn't old enough to drink or get into any clubs, so I guess they were just planning to hang on the beach all day and shop. I don't know, teenage girls always make grand plans and they really don't have a clue. But hey, that's the beauty of being a teenager I guess. Well anyway, just as I was getting back into my show, that stupid phone of mine started chirping. Of course it had to be somebody that I really didn't want to talk to.

"Hey," I answered

"Hey babe. What you doing?" Deon asked.

"I'm not your babe. What do you want? The kids are still with your mother," I said.

"I know. I just wanted to come over and chill with you for a while that's all," he replied.

"Chill? So what's your definition of chill? Especially at this time of night?"

"I just want to be in your company Rosie. I miss you."

"So you want to have sex. That's the underlying meaning of all that fluff you're talking right?"

"That's not what I meant but it would be nice," Deon said.

     The nerve of this guy. He really had a lot of balls calling me trying to get some, when he cheated on me not even a whole two months prior. Men I tell you. When they do something that they know is wrong, they expect to be forgiven with no hesitation. But let a woman do the same thing to them, they will act like it is the end of the world and hold it against that woman forever. For the life of me I just don't understand who made these rules. But anyway, I wanted to tell Deon no but at that moment my hormones were "jumping like a disco," in the words of Missy Elliot.

"OK you can come over for a little bit," I answered.

"For real?" he asked, surprised.

"Look stop acting dumb before I change my mind," I said.

     I hung up the phone even before he could get a chance to respond. I wasn't excited to see him, so I didn't even bother to get all cute and fancy for his visit. I kept on my cropped top and boy shorts, and I didn't even pull my hair down from the ponytail that it was in. He was lucky that I was even letting him come over at all. So I sat on the sofa watching TV until I saw Deon's car coming up the driveway on the security cameras. I watched him walk up to the door, and ring the doorbell. I decided that I would make him wait a few minutes before I

answered it. Why should I be rushing to the door to let him in? After about five minutes, my phone rang. It was him.
"Hello?"
"Rosie I'm at the door," Deon said.
"Oh for real? Did you ring the bell?" I asked giggling to myself.
"Yeah, like six times. I been standing out here for like ten minutes. Come open the door."
"OK here I come," I lied.

I watched him for another five minutes or so on the camera. He looked like he was getting pissed off, and I was loving it. Finally I got up from the sofa and opened the door for him.
"Damn what were you doing?" he inquired.
"None of your business," I remarked.

I walked back over to the sofa and sat down. I looked over at him and he handed me a bag.
"What's this?" I asked.
"I stopped and got you some of those lemon pepper wings that you like," Deon said.
"Oh," I said sitting the bag down beside me.
"So wassup?"
"Nothing."
"What's wrong?"
"Nothing."

Deon grabbed the bag of lemon pepper wings and put them at the other end of the sofa. Then he sat down beside me. All of a sudden I felt uncomfortable. Why did I tell him he could come over? I wasn't ready to be around him yet. I scooted in the opposite direction of him. He was too close.
"Why you treating me like I'm a stranger? What I can't sit next to you?" asked Deon.

Gosh he was so obnoxious! I didn't answer him, instead I continued to watch TV. And acted like I didn't hear what he said. Deon inched closer and closer, but I still pretended like he wasn't there. The next thing I knew he was all over me. Oh my goodness, I thought my hormones were raging before he came over, but once he started touching me I realized that they weren't. Well, they really were but the sight of his face was pissing me off.

"What are you doing?" I asked him.

"What do you think I'm doing?" he replied.

"What if V comes down here to get something to drink or eat or something?"

"Ard well let's go upstairs."

I got up and headed upstairs without responding. He was on me like white on rice. This man was acting like a dog in heat. Once we got in the room, he got my clothes of within a matter of seconds. This whole sexual encounter was giving me the creeps. Everything about it just felt wrong. He tried to kiss me and I turned my head. All I wanted was for it to be over. Once it finally was over, I was ready for him to go. He laid down beside me and turned over as if he was ready to get a good nights rest. But oh no, not on my watch. I had a trick up my sleeve for his cheating ass. I got up and put my robe on then tapped him on his back.

"What are you about to do?" I asked.

"I'm about to go to sleep, I had a long day. What you want me to stay up with you for a little while?" he asked.

"No, I want you to get your clothes on and go about your business," I remarked.

"What?"

"I know I didn't stutter."

"What's your problem?" he asked.

"I don't have a problem. I just think you should go home. We never discussed you staying the night," I remarked.

"So what's the problem with me staying? Everything was fine, and now you're acting crazy."

"So since I don't want your trifling cheating ass to stay the night then I'm acting crazy? Look you wanted to come over, and I was horny at the time so I said yeah because I'm not to the point where I feel like going out to find somebody new. I'm still married so I know that would be wrong for me to sleep with someone else. But that don't mean that I want you up in

here all comfy cozy like everything is cool between us because it's not," I explained.
"But I thought-"
"What? That we were back together? No, no, no... I never said that. Nope, I never said that," I interrupted.

    Deon looked at me like I was crazy. Treating him like a two dollar hoe was really making me smile on the inside. It was no way that I was going to let him come back that easily. I picked up his clothes and tossed them on the bed, then I left out of the room and went back downstairs. A few minutes later, Deon came stomping down the stairs. I was sitting on the sofa, eating my lemon pepper wings. Just because he was repulsive didn't mean that I had to let them good wings go to waste. He walked past me, not saying a word.
"Thanks for the wings!" I yelled to him before the door slammed.

    I laughed and continued to eat my food. Somebody was angry and it wasn't me. Oh well, good enough for him. I was glad that he was mad. That wasn't even a pinch of what I felt when I walked in that sun parlor and saw him laid up with that whore of a nanny. Good enough for him. I finished up my wings, took a nice hot shower and got in the bed . As soon as I started to doze off, my phone started to ring. It was Rochelle. I wondered what was going on, because she never called this time of night unless something was wrong.
"What's wrong?" I asked.
"They killed him!" she screamed into the phone.
"What? Who?"
"John John!"
"What? Oh Lord where are you?"
"Rose they shot him right in front of me! I'm so tired! I'm so tired of this! Why didn't they just kill me too?"
"Hold up Ro. Listen to me. Try to calm down. Tell me where you are," I said to Rochelle.
"I'm in the parking lot at Magnolia's," she cried.
"OK don't go nowhere I'm on my way," I told her.

I threw on a pair of leggings and a t-shirt then I grabbed my car keys and my purse. I didn't even bother to wake up Violet and tell her that I was leaving because she was going to have too many questions. I ran out of the house and jumped in the car. I had to get to my best friend, she was in distress and I needed to be there. I know I did at least eighty all the way there. When I pulled up, there were police every where, and there was the infamous yellow tape. I got out of the car and looked around. I spotted Rochelle, sitting on the ground in the middle of the lot.

I ran over to her and knelt down beside her. There was blood all over her clothes, and she was sweaty. I looked over to the other side of the lot and there he was, covered by a white sheet. Yup, he was dead. Ain't no coming from under that white sheet. My heart shattered into a million pieces.

"He is dead Rose! He is dead! What am I gonna do now? I know we didn't always get along but that still was my brother! And now look! He is gone! This shit just ain't right! Every time I turn around it's something else! My mother ain't even gonna be able to come to the funeral! I just don't know what to do!"

Tears poured from her bloodshot red eyes. I felt for Rochelle, I really did. She was the youngest of four, and the only girl. All her brothers and her father had been killed behind the drug game. This was truly sad. The even sadder part was her mother was in jail for organizing the hit on one of the guys who killed her father. All I could do was think about the times that I had gotten down on myself for the cards that I was dealt. I realized that there was always somebody out here who has it a little bit harder than you. True I lost my mother, but Rochelle had lost all of her immediate family. Sure I was going through a difficult time in my marriage, but Rochelle's mother was behind bars and she was going to be there for a very long time.

"It's OK Ro. I know you are hurting but I'm here for you. Come on, let's go home," I said.

I helped Rochelle off of the ground and we started to walk toward my car. Before we could even pull off, a police officer ran over to us and told Rochelle that a detective needed to get a formal statement from her at the station. I told her that I would drive her down there and I would wait for her. After she was done at the station, I took her back to her house, and I went in with her. I knew that she was going to need someone there with her. She cried all night, sometimes screaming and sometimes silently. I didn't like to see her like that. In fact, I had never seen her like that. Finally she fell asleep, so I decided to go to sleep too. Once the morning came, I got up before Rochelle and cooked breakfast. Just as I was finishing up Rochelle was walking into the kitchen.

"Good morning," she spoke.

"Hey Ro. How are you feeling?" I asked.

"Like I can't believe this is real. I just wish it was a nightmare and not real life."

"I'm so sorry Ro," I said.

No need to be sorry Rosie. But thank you for being here. It all just happened so fast."

"So what happened? If you don't mind me asking," I said.

"John John called me and asked me if I could come out with him to get a few drinks so we could talk. I told him yea. So he came and got me and we went to Magnolias. So he started talking about this life insurance policy that he has, and that I'm the beneficiary, and was just telling me all this stuff about where his money was and if something ever happened to him, how to divide his money up between his kids. So I asked him why was he talking about this all of a sudden and he was like no reason in particular, he just wanted to talk to me about it in person that's all. So I brushed it off as he just wanted to have that talk with me, since I was the closest one to him. So everything was cool, we had a good time. Everything was fine. Then when it was time to go, we were walking out and two dudes ran up to him and started shooting him.... Rose I was so scared. He fell on his face, and they ran off... I tried to pick him up off the ground but I couldn't.. People were running and screaming... I couldn't do nothing but hold him and scream for help," Rochelle cried.

All I could think was God is so good. John John was shot multiple times right beside Rochelle, and not a single bullet touched her. She made it out without a scratch. That was nothing but God. Not only that, these idiots opened fire in the midst of a whole crowd, and nobody else was hurt either. Everything happened for a reason, and truth be told, if you live by the sword you will die by the sword. It ain't but so many ways that you get out of that life. You either die, or go to jail. There are no fairy tale endings to that fast life. So if a person is in that life style, it's best to get out before it's too late. Unfortunately, John John didn't make it out. It really sucked that it had to be that way, but the game don't have favorites.
"Wow," I finally said.
"My mind just keeps rewinding back to the look on his face when he was talking about the life insurance policy. He wasn't telling me all that just so that I could know, he was telling because he knew he was going to get killed. Even when the dudes ran up on us, I looked at him and he didn't even look scared. He just closed his eyes. Rose he knew he was about to go. I wish he would've told me."
"I know... But he didn't want you to worry. You know it's a big brother's job to protect his little sister," I said trying to comfort her.
"I just don't get it Rose. Every time I turn around it's something else. I mean I don't think I'm a bad person.... I work, I look out for my friends, and I love my kids, so what's the problem? Why is there always something falling down on me? How much can a person take?"
"Sometimes God has to break you down so that he can draw you closer to him," I stated. "I'm not trying to preach to you, but you know I have been through a lot too. It wasn't until I got a relationship with God that I started to get some peace. There are some times when all I can think about is my mother, and no matter what I do I can't get her off my mind. But when I go to church and hear a sermon that seems like it was spoken just for me, or when I get on my knees and pray, it gets better. I'm telling you it will make you feel so much better."

"I don't do church, I keep telling you that Rose," Rochelle cried.

"Ro. I'm telling you what I know. When I'm going through something all week, and I can't see how I'm going to make it through, after I go to church on Sunday and I pray... and I cry.. and I hear the word of God... I feel so much better. It's like a weight it lifted off of me. Just go with me this Sunday. I'm telling you. If you open up your heart and let Him in, you will see the difference in your life," I tried to convince her.

"Church people are the phoniest ones," Rochelle came out of left field.

"There are phoney people everywhere Ro. That doesn't stop you from going out into the world now does it? No. I didn't think so. You don't go to church for the people. Forget them. It's not about them. That's not their house. The church is God's house."

Rochelle looked at me with so much pain in her eyes and she said, "My uncle was a pastor."

My heart skipped a beat. I finally understood why Rochelle was so against church. Now I knew why every time I even mentioned church Rochelle changed the subject. One of the people that is associated the most with the church is the pastor. So I got it. A person who was molested by a pastor would naturally have ill feelings against the church. It all clicked now.

"Rochelle, I know that hurts. You know I know first hand about how it feels to be violated. But you are an adult now, you are not a child anymore. No one can manipulate you into taking your body from you anymore. Every pastor out here is not a molester. A lot of them are good people. Nobody is perfect, don't get me wrong. But everybody isn't out to get you either. There is this bible verse I say to myself when I feel like life is getting the best of me. Be strong and of good courage, fear not, nor be afraid of them. For the Lord your God goes with you; He will never leave you nor forsake you. I know it's hard Ro, but you have to let your guard down a little bit. You can't keep doing the same thing and keep expecting different results. I want to see you happy. I want to see you have some piece of mind. But I'm not gonna push you either. I'm just extending an invitation. If you want to come with me one day, just let me know."

    Rochelle didn't say a word. My heart ached for my best friend. These sick people out here that prey on children just don't know how much they change that child's life forever. The sting of having your innocence taken away from you never goes away. It may get better with time, but it never goes away. Our silence was broken by Rochelle's phone ringing. I already knew what time it was. People were calling to ask about what happened to John John. After sitting through a few of them, I let Rochelle know that I would be going home to shower and change my clothes and that I would be back.

    The whole week leading up to John John's funeral was just a mess. He had eight children, with six different women. It seemed like every hour one of them was calling Rochelle asking for money or about his insurance policy or who was riding in the limo. I could tell that Rochelle was feeling down. Her daughter and son had moved to Atlanta with their dad after they had graduated from high school, and after they heard the news about their uncle they came up to Baltimore to be with their mother. That seemed to comfort her a little, but the constant nagging from those girls really didn't help.

    Once the day of the funeral came, I was relieved for Rochelle. I knew that after the funeral was over then a lot of the confusion would die down. Oh but the funeral itself was a pure circus. All types of women falling all over the casket and kissing John John in his mouth. People taking pictures in front of the casket. I mean this funeral was a ghetto hot mess. I sat next to Rochelle and held her hand. She sat there in a daze, not saying a word. After the funeral and burial was over, Rochelle wanted to go home. She didn't even want to be bothered with the repast and I totally understood. So I drove her home and she got in bed. I said a silent prayer for my best friend. I just wanted God to bring her out of this. Even the strongest person would lose their mind dealing with all that mess.

Sunday morning rolled around and I was so ready to go to church. I had a lot that I needed to leave at the alter. The grief of my Mama had crept back in, plus the grief I felt on behalf of my best friend was eating me up. Once I got there, I felt the dark cloud slowly moving away. Yes, the house of God was where I needed to be. While I was tapping my feet to the choir singing, my purse dropped on the floor. I bent down to pick it up and once I scooped up all my belongings and put them back inside, I felt a tap on my back. I looked up and Rochelle was sitting there beside me in the pew. I really wasn't expecting for her to show up to my church on a Sunday morning, but I was very happy that she did. This was a very pleasant surprise, and more evidence that God really answered prayers.

"Well hello there. Glad to see you here this morning," I said to Rochelle.

"I thought about what you said. I'm ready for some different results," she replied.

CHAPTER 19: Finding Out Where I Came From

I pulled up to the building and looked at the sign. Family Connections. Yup, this was it. I parked my car and went inside. I looked around as I walked up to the reception desk. Portraits of families were framed along the walls. I wondered if they were real families, or actors. You could never be sure these days. I mean my mother put on a act for years and I didn't even know it. I signed in on the sheet that had a pen on a string connected to it.

"How may I help you?" the receptionist asked.

What was the purpose of having a sign in sheet if you are going to just ask me what I'm there for anyway? That always puzzled me. But I wasn't there to give the receptionist a hard time, so I didn't bother to voice my opinion.

"I have a two o'clock appointment with Ms. Contessa," I answered back.

"OK, I will let her know that you are here. You can have a seat."

I sat down and immediately started to second guess my agenda. Was all this really necessary? Did I really need to know who my father was? I mean I was doing just fine without him. Before I could get up and leave a tall Hershey completed woman greeted me.

"Hi, are you Rose?" she asked.

"Yes," I said.

"It's nice to meet you. I'm Ms. Contessa. I spoke with you over the phone," she said extending her hand to me.

"Nice to meet you too," I said shaking her hand.

We went into her office and got straight to business. She wanted to know everything. But the crazy thing was, I didn't have much to tell her.

"My whole childhood I was lead to believe that my little sister's father was my father. It wasn't until after my mother's death that my aunt told me that he wasn't. My aunt doesn't have any information on this other guy, she doesn't even know who he is. I have my mother's last name, and there is no father listed on my birth certificate," I explained.

"OK. It's OK. We'll just have to dig a little deeper. Nothing is impossible," Ms. Contessa said.

"Really?"

"Nope. I have dealt with cases like yours before. But I will tell you that this is not going to be easy. We may run into a few dead ends, but I'm going to try my best to give you the answers that you need."

I left her office with a new found hope. Maybe I would finally find out where I came from. There was nothing wrong with at least trying. Like Rochelle said, everybody deserves to know where they came from.

Since Deon and I had separated, and when I had finally gotten out of my depression stage, I dived into my work head first. It hadn't even dawned on me that we had been separated for almost six months now. I had so many other things on my mind. The Christmas season had rolled back around and I couldn't help but to wonder how Elaina's kids were doing. I prayed that she had made a better life for them somewhere, but there was no way for me to tell. Maybe I could get Ms. Contessa to find them too. Naw, I wasn't going to do that. Elaina didn't want to be bothered with me, so I was going to just let her be. I had started to lose faith in Ms. Contessa anyway. She had called to give me an update that there weren't any updates. She hadn't gotten any closer to finding my father than she had on day one. Whatever.

So this one particular day, I was sitting at my desk, tying up some loose ends concerning my Rose Pedals line. My phone vibrated and I looked to see who it was. Unfortunately, it was Deon. What in the world did he want?

"Hello," I answered.

"Hey how are you?" he asked.

"I thought I asked you not to call this phone unless it was for the kids," I said.

"How do you know it's not?"

"Because they are in school and daycare and you know that."

"Rose you really need to stop it. This ain't for us."

"What do you want Deon?"

"So have you decided what you're doing for Summer's birthday?" he asked.
"Yeah. I'm taking them to Cali to Disney Land. I figured that would be cool."
"So you're doing Christmas over there too?"
"What kind of stupid question is that Deon? Ain't her birthday on Christmas?"
"Why you gotta be so smart Rose? I'm just asking questions so I can know what's going on."
"Well stop asking stupid questions and I won't give you smart answers," I remarked.
"So where are we staying Rose?" Deon asked.
"We?" I asked. "I didn't plan on you going."
"So you just excluded me and my family from my daughter's birthday?"
"No not you and your family, just you. I was going to invite them."
"You know what? I'm not about to keep kissing your ass. If you want to act like that, then that's fine. Don't worry about my family I will make all the arrangements for them."
"OK that's fine," I said un moved.

Deon hung up the phone in my ear and I could care less. I wasn't his mother, so I wasn't moved by his temper tantrums. He would be just fine and if he wasn't oh well that was his problem, not mine. Not even thirty seconds later my phone was vibrating again. This man just didn't know when to give up.
"What?" was how I answered the phone.
"I was really calling to ask you if you could go to court with me. I gotta go to the final custody hearing next week."

Wow. I had forgotten all about that. Deon was still trying to get full custody of Baby Deon permanently. But again, that wasn't my business anymore, I had my own life to worry about.
"Deon that's not my problem anymore. You deal with that. I was in your corner no matter what and you messed that up

when you decided to cheat. Go find Michelle and ask her to go to court with you."

"When is this going to stop Rose? You are my wife!"

"Like I said you should've thought about that when you were cheating. Now you have a nice day."

    I hung up the phone and went on about my day. I was way to busy to be tangled up with Deon and his mess. I had to get everything squared away for the official launching of Rose Pedals. I needed to do a photo shoot for the Lemon Wedge and Orange Slice shoe that I would be releasing first. Of course I booked Violet to be my cover girl. It just wouldn't have been right if I had done other wise. All I wanted to do was get this money. I didn't want to think about love or anything of that sort. The thought of Deon going on the trip for Summer's birthday made me ill. I was going to have to be in his presence for a whole week. I had a good mind to cancel the trip and to just go somewhere totally different and not tell anybody. But Miracle and Franko couldn't keep a secret to save their lives, and Deon would find out eventually and I wouldn't hear the end of it. Ever. So I put on my big girl drawers and went on with the original plan.

    It was Christmas Eve and everyone flew out to our trip destination like we had done the year before. Deon and his family were staying at the hotel right next door to where Rochelle, the kids and I were staying. Go figure. It was nice to see everybody, especially Man Man and Baby Deon. I really missed them and they had missed me too. They ran to me and gave me hugs and kisses once everybody met up for dinner. "They miss their family, and I do too. I'm ready to come home Rose," Deon whispered in my ear at the table.

    I ignored him because if I fed into his foolishness then it wouldn't be nothing nice. I was pissed that I had to even sit next to him. Everybody was pissing me off. Laughing and joking like everything was OK. Even Rochelle was talking to Deon like nothing was wrong. Hello! He cheated on me and I'm your best friend! Why are you talking to him? I hated Deon and I wanted the whole world to hate him too, even his own family. I know that was unrealistic, but that is really how I felt at that point. Every time I saw him a flash of that sun parlor scene replayed in my head, and I wanted to bash him upside his head. I had been so loyal to this man. I vowed to be faithful and true to him before God, and had said those same vows. Yet, he still broke them and threw everything away for some sleazy sex with someone that he didn't even know, yet care about. I still hadn't got past that. I wasn't sure if I ever could, and it was eating me up from the inside out.

   The tension was thick. More so on my end than his. Ms. Bonita would try to take pictures of us together with the kids and I would stand as far away from Deon as possible. When I had no choice to stand beside him he would try to put his arm around me and I would move it. I didn't need him getting any kind of mixed signals about this vacation. It was about the kids, and nothing more. One night I sat on my balcony sipping on a glass of wine just thinking about things. Rochelle came out on the balcony and sat next to me.

"Rose, you need to let it go," she said.
"What are you talking about?" I asked.
"The whole cheating incident."
"How can I let it go? This is my marriage we're talking about."
"You are letting it change you Rose. You are not the same at all," Rochelle responded.
"Oh well," I said.
"See that's what I mean. Your attitude is so nonchalant. Either it's that or you are extremely angry. What happened to the happy go lucky Rose? The Rose that used to smile? This whole time that we have been here all you do is frown. Your attitude is so rude and everybody is noticing it."
"I just want to be left alone. Thank you."
"So are you telling me to leave you alone?"
"Yes."
"OK. That's cool," Rochelle said before leaving the balcony.
   I heard my room door close, which meant that Rochelle had gone to her own room. Good. I really didn't feel like

hearing her opinions or her advice. Now it was safe. I could let go of that tough exterior. I could cry.

For the rest of the trip I stayed in my room and I sent the kids out with Deon and his family. I just wanted to go home. Going there with him was a big mistake and I should've just went with my gut instinct to cancel it. I didn't even want to breathe the same air as him. He was repulsive. The night before we left, I heard a knock on my door. I knew it wasn't the kids because we had an adjoining door, and Violet had a key.

"Rose please open the door we need to talk," I heard Deon say.
"No we don't, leave me alone," I replied.
"Rose please let me in."
"LEAVE ME ALONE I SAID!"

Finally he got the memo and he left. I started to pack up all of our things and I heard my phone ringing. It was Ms. Contessa. I really didn't feel like hearing any bad news, so I sent her to voice mail. I was over the whole finding my father thing at this point. My phone rang again right after that. Man his woman was persistent. So this time I answered.
"Hello."
"Hi Rose. This is Ms. Contessa. How are you?"
"I'm OK."
"Did I call you at a bad time?"

Now I'm not a genius or anything, but if a person sends you to voice mail then more than likely that means that they didn't want to talk right? This lady was something else.
"No it's fine. Just packing so that I can come home from vacation tomorrow," I said.
"OK. Well I'm sorry to interrupt so I'll make this quick. I found a name. It took a lot of digging and pressing but I found a name," she said.
"A name for what?" I asked.
"Your father's name."

It's like the world had stood still on it's axis for a few minutes. I really wasn't expecting for her to say that. My palms started to sweat, and my heart started to race. This couldn't be real.

"So what do I do now?" I asked.

"Nothing yet. I'm still trying to find an address or a telephone number on him, but I was just calling to let you know that we are making progress."

"Thank you so much," I said blinking back the tears.

"No problem. That's what I'm here for."

"Well keep me posted. Call me whenever you need to," I said.

"I will. But don't you even want to know what his name is?" Ms. Contessa asked with a chuckle.

"Oh yes, I'm sorry. I'm just so happy I really wasn't expecting this. So what's his name?" I asked.

"Juan Sanchez."

CHAPTER 20: Tuscany and Decisions

It was almost four months into the new year and more and more I had been entertaining the thought of filing for divorce. I thought I had carried the separation on long enough. And I was going to take Deon for all he had too. That would teach him not to step out on someone loyal ever again. But other than that, I was cool. Everything was going good with my businesses, and the kids were happy and healthy.

My day had been full with setting interviews up for my nannies and booking shoots for V. I was so glad that she had decided not to sign with a modeling agency. The both of us were truly eating. Violet's account was growing by the day, and mine was getting fatter as well. It felt good to be a black business woman. I was so blessed that I didn't have to work for anybody else. Stepping out on faith had brought me business opportunities one after another. It's nothing like doing what you love. When you decide that you want to go into business for yourself, there will always be people that will look at you like you are crazy. But that's OK, you can't expect everyone to see your vision. Some people are OK with working a nine to five, and there is nothing wrong with that. But there others like me, who instead of building the bank account of someone else, would rather make them selves wealthy. I feel really bad for those who work a job day in and day out, and are miserable. Thank God that I followed my inner voice that told me to go for it. And now I was in a position to show my sister and my kids how to build their own empires as well, because at the end of the day, that's who I was doing all this for, my family. I wanted them to be able to live comfortably when I was dead and gone, and not just for a few months off of a life insurance policy either.

I decided to go to lunch for some good food and clarity. I needed to step away from my work for a little bit and have some me time. So I grabbed my car keys and headed out. Before I got in the car I remembered that I needed to check the mailbox. I went to the mailbox and opened it. There weren't any bills which was a plus, but there was an envelope with my name written on it. I knew that handwriting from anywhere. Deon still hadn't laid off of the apology gifts, and I had been tired of them. If he didn't get it by now then I didn't know when he would. He was not going to be able to buy his way back in. I was at a point in my life where anything I wanted to have or do, I could afford myself. If this was a few years back then maybe I would've been flattered, but not now. I opened up the envelope and there were two plane tickets and a brochure for Fonteverde, a five star resort in Tuscany. I looked at the brochure and I must admit, it was a very nice resort. All inclusive, so you wouldn't have to go anywhere unless you really wanted to. I really wasn't in the mood to be vacationing but when I really thought about it, Rochelle deserved one. Even though we had been in Cali in December, that was a trip for the kids and I hadn't been the most pleasant person to be around. She had been working really hard, and the tragedy with her brother had really taken a toll on her. So I figured a trip to Italy would cheer her up a bit. When I told her about the trip, she was so excited.

"Girl you must've been giving him the business! A trip to Tuscany for an apology gift? Even after you keep treating him like garbage! Bitch you living large and in charge!" Rochelle yelled into the phone.

Now that's the Rochelle that I knew lively and crazy as hell. Yes indeed it was time for a girls trip, just her and I. I couldn't wait to see what we would get into.

The first class flight to Italy was marvelous darling. No lay overs and completely comfortable. Deon sure did know how to treat a girl who was about to file for divorce. When we got to our resort, we decided to go have lunch pool side. Just as Rochelle and I had started to dig into our food, my phone rang. I looked at it, but I didn't recognize the number. I didn't feel like entertaining any conversations other than the one that I was having with Rochelle, but it could've been somebody trying to book Violet. I decided to answer.
"Hello?"
"Hi Rose," the voice on the other end said.

I took a deep breath. I could recognize that voice from anywhere. What could she possibly want from me?

"Is there a reason that you are calling me?"

"We need to talk," Ms. Nancy said.

"About what?"

"I know I was wrong for what I said to you. I was completely out of line. But I miss being in my grand children's lives. I want to see them."

Well hold on. Let me catch yall up on this situation. I had stopped speaking to Ms. Nancy around the time that Deon and I had gotten engaged. She had went on this whole tangent about how I was moving on too fast, and I was just trying to find a replacement father for Miracle and Franko. Then to top it all off, she said that if I went through with the marriage that she didn't want anything to do with it. So I completely cut her off. I didn't have time for that negativity. So in a nutshell, I hadn't heard from her since then. Now all of a sudden this lady was calling me talking about she missed her grand kids. Really? After all this time?

"Ms. Nancy, really I don't have a problem with you. I just have a problem with the things that you say out of your mouth. No matter what I am their mother. That is something that you can't change. I am always going to have their best interest at heart, and I'm gonna do what's best for them. So it's not your place to try to tell me how to live my life."

"I understand that and again I apologize," she said.

"Well look. Right now isn't the best time for me to be talking about this, I'm on vacation in Italy... So I guess I will talk to you when I get back home," I remarked.

"Oh OK," she responded sounding all dumb.

"I know that wasn't who I think it was," Rochelle said sipping her wine.

"Yup. People kill me when they want to pop back in years later with their apologies," I said as I took a sip of mine.

"Yeah that's crazy. But maybe she's being genuine."

"Maybe, maybe not." But I'm not about to be trying to figure that out right now. She's not even that important."

"I feel you. So what's going on with finding your father?"
"Not much. Still haven't found anything else out but his name," I said.
"And that name is crazy. Juan Sanchez though?"
"I know right," I laughed.
"Wouldn't it be crazy if he was Mexican or something?" Rochelle asked.
"Yea, it would be. But I don't think so. I think he's black and his mother was eating tacos when she had him."
"I thought I said some crazy stuff out of my mouth," Rochelle laughed. "But when you find him, what you think you're gonna say to him?"
"*If* I find him Imma be like..... Nigga, where the hell you been at?"

We both bust out laughing. The view was beautiful. This was the life. Sharing this beautiful vacation with my best friend, away from all our problems. I wished everyday could be like this.
"I think it's about time I move on," I said to Rochelle.
"Where you moving?"
"I'm talking about Deon girl. I think it's time to move on."
"Girl yeah right. Yall two are meant to be together. You just need a little more time to cool off," Rochelle replied.
"Ro it's almost been ten months. I really think I'm ready to file for divorce and start dating."
"Divorce? Dating? Girl it's real out here. That dating game ain't nothing to mess with, I'm telling you right now."
"Well how else am I going to get to know somebody? I'm gonna have to date in order to see what I like and what I don't," I responded.
"Oh OK... Well go ahead and knock yourself out. Get you an Italian man while you're here."
"Um. I don't think so."
"Come on girl don't discriminate!" Rochelle laughed.
"Whatever," I replied.
"Naw but seriously, if you really want to go on a date I got somebody for you."

" Oh my goodness. Who is it?" I asked.
"Why you say it like that?" Rochelle laughed.
"Because you know some crazy dudes that's why."
"Girl please. Look, his daughter comes to me for tap lessons. He always is dressed nice, and he always pays on time, so I know he has a job. I've never seen a ring on his finger, and he seems pretty nice. I think he would be a good match for you," Rochelle replied.
"How do you know he's single?" I asked.
"I don't but I'm going to find out once we get back."
"Whatever Rochelle," I said sipping my wine.
"Girl please I'm definitely gonna set yall up because you need some bad," she laughed again.

      For the rest of the trip, we were treated like royalty. Daily massages, wine tastings, and shopping sprees all compliments of Deon. I was starting to think that maybe I wasn't so ready after all. Any other man would've gave up and moved on. Deon could have any woman that he wanted literally. Since they had won the Super Bowl two years in a row, Deon was the highest paid quarterback in the NFL. But no matter how bad I treated him, I still got a daily "I love you" text from him. He was still showering me with apology gifts ten months after I made him leave. He was still a great father to Summer and to my kids who weren't even biologically his. I really had a lot to think about. Maybe I had made him suffer enough.... Nah.

      When it was time to go home, I really didn't want to. Italy was truly a breath of fresh air. Our trip was great, we had a very good time. But it was time to get back to our lives. Once we got back to Baltimore, I felt a sense of relief like I always did when I got back in town.... I guess that's how it is when you have a comfortable home to come back to. Ms. Bonita brought the kids home, and I thanked her for keeping them while I was away. It was time for me to get back to work. My mind drifted back to the conversation that I had with Rochelle in Italy about being ready to move on. I secretly wished that Rochelle was just playing about setting me up with the guy that brought his daughter to her class. I thought that I was ready to date, but I realized that I really wasn't. Unfortunately, my wish didn't come true. Three days after getting back from Italy, she was calling me talking about "she set something up." His name was Bruce and he was single. I didn't want her to get any hint that I had been missing Deon, because that would make me look soft, so I just went along with it. He texted me the next day, and we agreed to meet at the Blue Dolphin Saturday evening at eight o'clock. It seemed like I blinked twice and Saturday was here. I was so nervous it had been ages since I had been out on a date with anyone besides my husband. After changing my outfit about five times, I was finally ready. I decided on my black tank dress that fit me like a glove, and my red peep toe pumps, with a red clutch and silver accessories. It was drizzling outside so I couldn't possibly wear my hair straight, I would have a bush before I got to the car. So I pulled it up into a bun and put on some red lipstick. Voila! I was ready to go on my date. Just the thought of it sounded funny. But anyway, I left Violet on baby sitting duty with pizza and wings to snack on for the night. I made my way out of the door praying that everything would go alright.

  The date started off OK. When I got there he was already there, and had us a table. He was very easy on the eyes as well. Very dark, but his complexion was as smooth as butter. He had dreads that hung down to he middle of his back, and they were very neat. Not a hair was out of place. But when he started to talk, the date quickly went south. For the first twenty five minutes he talked my head off about himself. What college he went to, his grade point average when he was there, his favorite shoe store, and then his favorite football team... Which just so happened to be the Ravens. What had I signed up for? I was on a date with a crazed Raven's fan. This just couldn't be real.

"I used to see you all the time when they used to cut the camera over to you during the games," Bruce said.

"Oh really?" I asked as if I cared.

"Yea... So it must be nice being able to stay home and still be rich," he stated.

"Um, well actually I don't stay home. I have my own daycare center, I have my own business where I appoint nannies to celebrity clientele, I have my own shoe line, and I manage my little sister Violet. She's the face for Youth perfume," I verbalized.

"Oh well damn. You're just doing the damned thing!" he chuckled. "See if I were you, I would just sit home and chill. I wouldn't even work myself to death. I would just reap the benefits. You got kids don't you? Please I would just live in the lap of luxury without a care in the world. You are so lucky."

"First of all, my husband has money, but that's his money. If I wanted to stay home, then I could. But I choose not too. I want my own. Nothing that belongs to someone is else is guaranteed to you. Period. I have to be able to stand on my own two feet. And for the record I don't believe in luck. So the term would be blessed, not lucky. But I'm also blessed with so many opportunities to do so many big things for myself, that I'd be a fool not too."

"Well yeah. To each it's own I guess," he remarked.

Me oh my. This man was so clean cut, but he was a straight up retard. I couldn't believe that I was actually in this situation. I was sitting across the table from a straight up jack ass. I prayed that this date would be over sooner than later. Once our entrees were brought to us, I couldn't help but notice this funny feeling that I was having. Something wasn't right, but I just couldn't put my finger on it. So I sat at the table with Bruce, pretending to care about the conversation.

"So, you manage your sister right?" Bruce asked.

"Yup. She's doing really well to be so early in her career. I'm really proud of her," I said with a smile.

"Wow. I know that has to be cool. You get to travel, and I bet she's making a lot of money."

Now I knew I wasn't hearing things... This idiot had the audacity to ask me a question about the money that my sister was making? He couldn't be serious. That was strike one.

"Yes the travel is nice, but I'm more excited for her, not for me," I said.

"So what's it like being married to a NFL star?"

Pause. Did he just ask about Deon? This dude really didn't know when to quit! Did he really want to date me, or was he just a groupie? I was really starting to believe that he was a groupie. I shook my head in disbelief. Strike two.

"I'll be right back, I have to use to excuse myself to the ladies room," I said avoiding his question.

I speed walked to the restroom and pulled out my phone. I dialed Rochelle's number. Once she answered, I didn't even give her a chance to speak.

"I 'm just calling you to let you know that I am going to kill you," I said.

"Why? What I do?" she asked.

"Girl don't act dumb you set me up with this damn Looney Toon! All he keeps talking about is what type of money we are making and about Deon! His ass is star struck!"

"How was I supposed to know? He seemed like a cool guy. He was always so respectful when he dropped off Kya to class. He ain't seem like a groupie. You said you wanted a regular guy, and he's a regular guy so..."

"So nothing! Look. In ten minutes, I need you to call me and say that I have an emergency at home so I can get the hell out of here!"

"Damn. He must really be a nut," Rochelle laughed.

"I'm glad you think it's funny because I'mma put my foot up your ass when I see you. Don't forget. Ten minutes. Bye."

I could still here Rochelle laughing as I hung up the phone. I couldn't believe that she set me up with this fool. I took a deep breath and went back to the table. I sat down and tried to finish up my dinner, counting down the minutes in my head for Rochelle to call me. Bruce talked my head off, and I just wanted to go home.

"So since technically since you're still married to him, you still get to go to the games for free right?"

Oh no this fool didn't! Strike three. I put my fork down on my plate and just as I was about to give this dummy a piece of my mind, my phone rang.
"Yes," I thought.
She was right on time. Ten minutes exactly. I got prepared to do some acting as I picked up the phone.
"Hello?"
"Girl you got an emergency come home right away," Rochelle laughed in my ear.
"Why what's going on?" I asked in my pretend voice of concern.
"I don't know didn't tell me what else to say," Rochelle continued to laugh.
"OK... I'm on my way," I said before I hung the phone up.
"Is everything OK?" Bruce asked.
"Um.. Not really. My baby sitter has to go, she had an emergency.. So I have to get home," I lied.
"Your husband is here," Bruce said.
"What?" I asked.
"Your husband is here," he repeated himself.
"Where?"
"Right there," Bruce said pointing to the window.
I froze up like a statue. As if the situation wasn't awkward enough he was making it even more awkward. I wanted to turn around and look, but at the same time I didn't. This was some real life crazy stuff. What in the world would possess him to show up while I was on a date? For his own sake he better not embarrass me, because anybody who knows me knows that I hate to be embarrassed. Doing so might result in you getting your head knocked off. I slowly turned my body and there he was, standing at the window behind my table, motioning me to come outside. I decided that I would ignore him. I turned back around and tried to focus my attention back on Bruce. Before I could say anything he interrupted me.
"He's coming in," Bruce said.
"Oh my goodness," was the only reply that I could think of.

I grabbed my purse and pulled out a wad of cash, not even sure how much it was. I knew it was more than enough to cover the bill though.
"Here. This should cover the bill. I have to go," I said, placing the money on the table.
"Oh.. OK," he said.
Bruce picked up the money and started to peel through the bills. His eyes were wide as saucers. I didn't even care if it was more than what was needed for the bill. I was just trying to get the hell out of there. Before I could scoot my chair from underneath the table, Deon was right there staring in my face.
"Can I talk to you for a minute?" he asked.
"I really don't think this is time or the place for this," I responded.
"Well when will it be? I tried to get you to come outside but you ignored me. I call your cell phone and you ignore me. I call the house phone and you ignore me. I try to talk to you when I come get the kids and when I drop them off but you wont talk to me then. So when is it going to be the right time?"
"I don't know, but not right now."
"Rose I know that I messed up. But I can't go another day without you. You are my everything, I love you more than anything. You are my soul mate. I miss you, I miss being in the same household with the kids. I know that it is going to take a lot for you to trust me again, but I am willing to do whatever it takes for that to happen. I don't want a divorce. I don't want my family to be broken up. I want my family back, whatever you want me to do I will do it. Just let me come back home. Please let me come back home."
At first I didn't know what to say. I wanted to be mad at him, but the truth was I really wasn't mad anymore. And to be even more truthful, I missed Deon. I really did. I missed his smiles and his warm embraces. I missed him holding me at night. I missed eating dinner with him and the kids together. I was tired of fighting, I felt like I had made him suffer long enough. He did something that he shouldn't have, and I had

made him pay. It was killing him to see me on a date with another man. Enough was enough. I wanted my husband back. Deon got down on one knee in front of me. He pulled out my wedding band and put it back on my finger. Then he pulled another ring box out of his pocket. When he opened it up I was damn near blinded.
"Like I said. I'm ready to come home. I want to renew our vows. I want to do any and everything you want me to do to make this right. Don't you miss me?"
　　By this time everyone in the restaurant was looking at us. I could feel my face getting flushed. As much mouth as I have, I still hadn't said a word. I had to digest his every word, because I had to be sure that he wasn't playing around.
"So can I trust you? Can I feel comfortable with going out of town? Can I be okay with you going away for work without worrying about what you're doing? I have been true to you in this marriage. That's all I ask for in return," I said finally.
"Yes you can. I want you I don't want nobody else. I need you back in my life Rosie I'm begging you," he said laying his head in my lap.
"Take him back girl," a lady at a table across the room said.
"Mind your business," the guy who was with her said.
　　I looked at them and smiled. People loved to see a happy ending in the movies, and in real life.
"OK," I finally said.
"Huh?" Deon asked lifting his head from my lap.
"I said OK. You can come home."
　　Deon sprung to his feet and picked me up from the chair, embracing me so tightly it was kind of hard to breathe. I guess he really did miss me. He put me down and kissed me so deeply, that I damn near melted onto the floor.
"I don't mean to interrupt yall but, can I get your autograph?" Bruce asked Deon.
　　We stopped kissing, looked at each other, and busted out laughing. We walked out of the restaurant hand in hand, leaving Bruce at the table by himself. Thank God that he came and saved me from this ratchet mess of a date! Poor Bruce. He

just couldn't get it right. I wonder where he is now. Probably somewhere trying to date another football player's wife while they are separated. Hahahaha that was one crazy ass dude. When we got home, the kids were so happy to see Deon. My heart was filled with so much joy. Things were finally back to normal. It was killing me to be without him, but I had to do what I had to do. Violet gave Deon a hug.

"About time, I was starting to get worried," she said with a smile.

"Me too," Deon replied.

Trina dropped Man Man off to the house. I was surprised when she actually opened up her mouth to talk to me. "I'm glad yall are back together, because he was one sad looking nigga when yall wasn't," she said before she pulled off.

Deon's mother brought Baby Deon over too. The house wasn't quiet until after two a.m. We laughed, played video games with the kids, and just enjoyed each others company. Our clan was back to being a complete unit. Yes indeed, everything was back to how it should be. After the kids finally conked out, it was time for the man and woman of the house to kiss and make up. Deon wasn't lying when he said that he missed me. He touched every spot just the way that he was supposed to. He kissed me from the top of my head to the soles of my feet. I think he was subconsciously communicating to me that this is what I would have been missing if I would've divorced him. I heard his silent language loud and clear. I must say, that was truly a night to remember.

CHAPTER 21: Juan Sanchez

    I picked up the phone and listened silently as she told me that she had finally found a phone number with a match to my father's name. I had been praying that this would finally happen, but honestly I never really expected it to.
"Hello, are you still there?" Ms. Contessa asked.
"Yes, I'm here."
"Are you OK?"
"Yea, just a little shocked that's all," I replied.
"That's understandable. But if this is really what you want then you have to take the first step. And if you decide that you're not ready that's fine too. It's OK to be afraid though."
"Yea I know. I'm just trying to process it," I responded. "But thank you. I really do thank you for helping me. It's crazy because I think that in the back of my mind I was kind of hoping that you never found him, so that I wouldn't have to live this moment that I am in right now."
"No it doesn't sound funny at all. It sounds real. That's usually how it goes when you want something so bad. You start to believe you actually don't. Life is full of puzzles and oxymorons. But like I said before, if you're not ready it's OK. No one can make you do this. It's up to you."

    I sat at in my room, thinking long and hard. I was scared to death. Ever since I had found out that Leon wasn't my father, I wanted to know who really was. Finally I had the chance to find out, and I wasn't sure if I wanted to. Why didn't he try to find me? What if he didn't want to find me? That's when I realized that I wasn't gonna know the answers to either of those questions until I reached out to him. I had nothing to lose in this situation, so I had to suck it up and go with the flow. I took a few deep breaths and dialed the number. It began to ring and my heart was in my throat. I hung up. I was too

scared. I took a few more deep breaths, and then I got down on my knees and closed my eyes. I began to speak.
"Father God I come to you as humble and sincere as I know how. First I want to thank you for all that you have done thus far. I want to thank you for the many blessing that you have given my family. I want to thank you for bringing my marriage back together, and for helping me to forgive. I want to ask forgiveness for all my sins, for everyone who I have hurt intentionally and unintentionally. But father in the name of Jesus now I need you more than ever. I am afraid Lord. I am terrified. I asked and I received and now I am unsure Lord. Please give me the strength to go forth and seek out my earthly father. Please Lord, what ever your will is, please let it be done. Please continue to keep your hand over me and my family. In Jesus name I pray. Amen."

  I got up from the floor and grabbed the phone and dialed the number again, and again it started to ring.
"Hola," the woman said.
  I was taken aback. Did I dial the wrong number? I looked at the number on the paper then at the phone to see if I had dialed correctly. OK, so I did dial the right number.
"Hola," she spoke again.
"Um, hola? May I speak to Juan Sanchez?" I asked.
"Que?"
  Oh my goodness. This is where my Spanish class would've did me some good if I had actually paid attention. This lady didn't know what I was talking about.
"Juan Sanchez?" I asked.
"Un momento," she answered back.
  I heard her sit the phone down. I was hoping that maybe she was going to get him or something. This was just too crazy for words. I listened hard and started to hear a conversation in the background.
"Alguien esta en el telefono para ti," I heard her say.
"Asi que es?" I heard in a man's voice.
"No se' que estan hablano Ingles," she answered back.

After a little more of their back and forth Hispanic talk, finally he came to the phone.

"Hello, yes this is Juan," the man on the phone said with a mild accent.

Oh my gosh. Rochelle was right. Now how in the world did my mother get hooked up with an immigrant? This was too much, too fast.

"Juan Sanchez?" I asked.

"Yes," he replied. "And you are?"

"Rose. Rose Peers. I'm calling because I... Well I'm your-"

"My daughter. I know who you are."

I didn't know what to say. He actually knew who I was, which meant that he knew I existed. So why hadn't he reached out to me?

"I knew that this day would come. God finally saw fit for us to meet," he said.

"I guess so."

"Well..... I guess we have some catching up to do huh?"

"Yeah..... Looks like we have a lot of catching up to do," I said to my father.

Made in the USA
Columbia, SC
08 September 2021